WONDROUS JOURNEY

The World is Waiting for You

WONDROUS JOURNEY

The World is Waiting for You

by Dean W. Jacobs

Travel 4 Life
Fremont, Nebraska   USA

Good Journey

Wondrous Journey
The World is Waiting for You
© 2004, by Dean W. Jacobs

1st Edition
2004

ISBN 0-9749441-0-6

Travel 4 Life
2040 East 22nd Street
Fremont NE 68025 USA

Printed in United States of America, 2004

This book is dedicated to my father;
Charles "Windy" Jacobs,
who was a traveler and storyteller in his own right.

And,
to all those who have ever looked at
a soaring plane, train or bus
and felt a tug in their hearts to go explore.

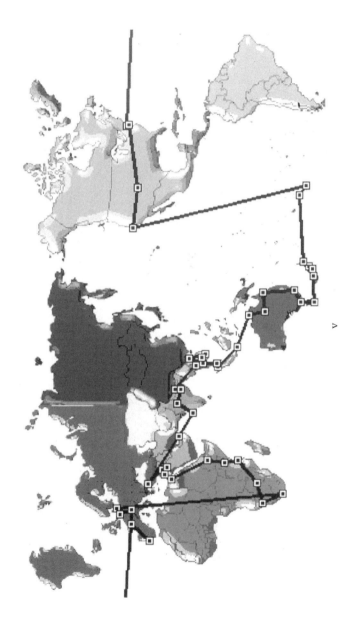

Acknowledgements

There are a number of people I would like to recognize who have supported me in this journey and adventure.

•First is my brother Dale, who made sure my life continued to run in my absence, allowing me to relax and know if it could be handled, it would.

•My family and friends that followed me vicariously each step along the way, sending me emails of encouragement to keep going.

•Special thanks to Dr. Paul Campbell and Gary Blinn, who first planted the seeds of travel when I didn't have the money or courage.

•All the traveling companions I had along the way with whom I shared endless bus hours, train rides, rickshaws, walks, talks, food, mosquito-filled rooms, sidewalk food stalls, crammed minivans, taxis, trucks and boats. One of the greatest rewards of travel is the endless encounters with fellow travelers who add wonderful color to the journey. I name you in my heart with a prayer of gratitude.

I especially want to thank and express my gratitude to all those who offered me such kindness, respect and generosity during my journey.

•The local people who smiled at my singing and the children with whom I danced the Hokie Pokie.

•Those who pored through my photos, seeking a glimpse of America.

•The people who took me by the hand to make sure I found the right bus, street, restaurant, hostel or bathroom.

•There are endless beautiful scenes in the world; it is the smiles of those who live there that add the true richness to a journey. I shout your names to the heavens that you may be blessed forever.

And finally I give thanks to the Divine, who led me each and every step of the way trusting that I was ready for the lessons unfolding before and within me.

Most of my life I have thought about writing a book. It is one thing to think about writing a book, but a totally different thing to actually create it.

•I thank my editors, Steve and Annie Wamberg, whose magic brought life to the dream.

•Marty Shull did what all the king's horses and men couldn't do for Humpty Dumpty by putting all the pieces together.

•Jared McCarthy of McCarthy Creative brought the project a book cover that truly captures the wonder of the journey.

And all those who believed in me, thank you for the gift.

Introduction: The Start

I believe we all have the innate desire to understand and know more about the world in which we live. In turn, we hope that knowledge will produce a better understanding of ourselves.

Each of us has a different expression of this desire, but I contend each of us is born with it. Maybe that's why, for these thousands of years of recorded history, people of all ages have left on quests and pilgrimages in search of various treasures. The best stories from these quests prove that the greatest treasure lies within your own heart. These are the tales that reflect how someone develops character and self-understanding in response to their journeys.

But those stories never happen if you sit down to wait for the world to come to you. The treasure is rarely a product of open-heart surgery. It is something which each of us must find in our own unique way. It allows us to discover those doors that open to reveal the treasure within.

I also have a sense that we have lost the nobility and honor that comes from such a journey. We have 45-year-old executives who, emotionally and spiritually, are behind their ten-year-old children. They have all the "adult toys" of life, but none of the real joys. It is no wonder they are frustrated with life, and make life hell for those around them.

I am no scientist, but I have a theory. You might interpret it to be sexist, but it is not intended to be that way. My theory is this: in order for a boy to become a man he must experience a certain degree of risk and fear—not imaginary, but real. This experience triggers a chemical change in a young man which allows him to move into becoming a man. It's not the final stage of passage—there are enough books already written on that, anyway—but an important one that has been celebrated by mankind in all cultures since the beginning of recorded time.

Consider the wilderness time spent alone by adolescent males in some Native American cultures, or the first solo hunt that marked a boy's passage from childhood into manhood for other societies. What is our equivalent in today's society? Carving our names into video games at arcades? We are missing these visceral rites of passage—something that reminds one of one's place in the world, and the challenges of life—in today's society. The proof lies in the immature actions of adults.

In the past, wars provided this kind of experience for some cultures. But the nature of war has changed and, besides, it must be possible to have this experience without creating needless suffering.

Again, this is only my theory. Maybe some day, some researcher will go looking to measure some kind of hormone that demonstrates the change, and validates these rites of passage. Until then, we have only a long history of cultures pointing in that direction, the desire to go and seek adventure. As best I can tell, you cannot experience it through a movie or at Disney World, either. It has to be real.

My adventure served in some ways as this rite of passage for me. I had every cultural indicator that I was an adult in my society. Our measurements, after all, are predatory behavior in the business world and the spoils thereof. But that feeling that there was more, a greater story for me to tell, haunted me until I was well into the adventure I'm about to share with you.

I am not a writer, either. I'm just a storyteller that decided to follow his heart and go on this journey. If you are looking for deep intellectual thought, this book is not going to be for you. However, if you're looking to read about what it is like to leave everything you know behind in order to discover things you haven't even heard of before, then come along and take this journey with me.

These are the observations of a man rediscovering his dream and love of travel, of taking risks to see what might happen, and trusting his heart each and every step of the way to see what hidden lessons were to be learned. I fully appreciate that not all of us can just walk away from our lives and take a journey for 22 1/2 months without creating a big mess. I did because I could.

And those who can have a great responsibility to do just that. If we are ever going to have a world that will live in some kind of peace, it will come from people like you and me who are willing to take the risk and sit face-to-face, across the table, with others from new and different cultures to share our humanity. Most of the world will never have the money for that journey. Many of you adults reading this right now do. And this could be one of our greatest legacies, to reach out with our own hands and share our lives with others across cultures, and commit together to build a just and peaceful world.

Hmmm. That sounded deep for a moment. But I mean it. And whether you agree with me or not on that point, this book will let you see what it's like to live out of a backpack for two years. You can find out how far one can really go on a small budget as a world traveler, and what kind of strange situations you can get yourself into.

In any case, may the pages that follow someday inspire you to take your own leap across the border!

Dean Jacobs
Fremont, Nebraska
December 2003

Entry One: *Where to begin*

I'd spent years simplifying my life. The natural next step was to leave my job and travel the world, right?

Once that decision was made, I immediately made two purchases. First, I found a new travel hat that seemed to suit the journey I was about to take. Second, I bought a new Rand McNally world map.

I spread the map out on my bed and started dreaming. *I can go anywhere I want. Where do I begin? What have I always wanted to see?*

Traveling the world. I'd always felt I'd need to win the lottery or marry rich to make it happen. I grew up in a modest, lower-middle income family. My father was a truck driver, my mother a housewife. We never had that much. As an adult, I'd worked pretty hard to accumulate a certain amount of wealth. So what I was about to do went against some very deep insecurities that were planted in me so long ago.

But I was determined to follow my heart. I needed to pass through whatever fears that were attempting to short-circuit my dream. I started putting dots on the map, marking my dream destinations that combined—until now—were nothing more than a well-worn fantasy. (As it turned out, there were other destinations that had been "dream spots" for so long that I'd completely forgotten about them until I was already on the road.)

New Zealand and Australia felt so far away and distant. It seemed that it would take forever just to get there, let alone see anything. If I ran out of time, energy or money I definitely wanted to have seen New Zealand and Australia, so they went at the top of the list. After that? I've always liked Thai food, so Thailand seemed the logical choice.

The U.S. has a history with Vietnam. My love of the mountains put Nepal on the list after that. Then came India, mostly because of its amazing and diverse spirituality. After that it was a dot on Turkey. Israel would let me see the Holy Land, and Egypt the Pyramids. Then I put a dot on Africa. I was clueless about where to go there, but I knew I at least had to see Victoria Falls and go on safari. The last dots went on South America: the Amazon River, the Patagonia Mountains, Machu Pichu of Peru, then up through Central America and home.

As with any planned trip, I made it to many of these destinations—but not all of them. That being said, I also made it to many places I'd never dreamed I would. I kept open to new ideas and new routes. I had no real time frame. My only real limitation was that when the money ran out, I'd have to go home. My budget plan was simple: I'd spend as little as possible, but still meet the trip's objectives.

I wanted to see things and explore. I wanted this journey to take me off the beaten path on my own, with my own timing and at my own expense. I intrinsically knew that a cheap budget would put me in closer contact with the "everyday people" in a country. That's who I was most interested in meeting, anyway. I thought things through enough to avoid backtracking whenever possible. Backtracking, in my view, was a waste of time. I started with a route and plan, but let go of any concepts or attachments as to how it might unfold.

Finally, I walked into a San Francisco travel agency to help me connect the dots on the Rand McNally. The reality began to sink in that I was about to embark on a real journey, not just another holiday getaway. The people I worked with at Airtreks, who specialize in this kind of traveling, were great. They helped me connect the dots, and suggested routes that I would have never thought of attempting. The first suggestions were stopovers at the Cook Islands and Fiji. And why not? I could do this for $40 each stop. It was a bargain especially knowing that, most likely, I would never be there again.

I took advantage of that marvelous deal, and so the journey began.

Entry Two: Island life

I boarded Air New Zealand and took off for the Cook Islands. When it was first suggested to me, I had the hardest time finding the Cook Islands on the map. But the location sounded cool. In fact, I was leaving winter in the Northern Hemisphere and was heading there for winter. I wanted a little warm sunshine.

Somehow, I had accidentally left my walking stick at the LA airport. The thought of it upset me because I had spent a great deal of time training with that stick. For months I had taken a martial arts course and in some classes had learned how to use it as a pretty good weapon. It wasn't meant to be, and was my first lesson in letting go of how I thought things should be.

Well, island life offered a good rhythm for me to begin the journey. The frantic pace that was kept up right until the time of departure faded away into a relaxing pace of, "What will I do today?" On the plane ride, I started reading about the Cook Islands only to find out that it's a law to have a place booked before you land. (Whoops, that one got by me.) I fudged my way through that, and found a hostel perfect for a home base as I explored the island.

It took a bit to get used to driving a scooter on the left side of the road, but since there were mainly scooters there, it was pretty safe. I walked across the island through the mountains in three and a half hours. That will give you a sense of how small it is!

The people were warm and beautiful, the government was a bit corrupt, and the island is a natural stopping place for those traveling across the Pacific. So you get all kinds here.

I attended a local church. The singing in Maori was so passionate, and loud enough for the heavens to hear—not hard to understand with the warm blue skies, crystal clear water, and quiet moments on the beach!

The Cook Islands offered several islands to go explore, but that all took money that I wasn't willing to part with. So, after ten days of soaking up sun and snorkeling, I headed for Fiji for more of the same—but at less expense.

Island life photograph   [1], page 91

Entry Three: Fiji

The adventure of navigating into a new and foreign place begins the moment you walk out of customs. After the usual money exchange in Nada, Fiji, my two temporary traveling companions (Carl from Finland and Melissa from California) and I found the express bus to Suva where we spent the night before heading out to Leleuvia Island.

Suva was very quiet. We didn't have any problems, except for a taxi that attempted to charge us double (we were pre-warned) and someone who tried to pickpocket Carl. It was so humid that your clothes never dried. It was just plain sticky, and they refused to let me into the local water hole because I wore shorts. Strange law.

Everyone was very friendly, wanting to know your name and where you came from. They said "hello" to you—actually, they yelled at you saying "bulla" as you walked on the other side of the street.

From Suva, we took a taxi to Bau Landing to catch a boat that would ferry us out to the small island of Leleuvia. Leleuvia is a tiny island, so small that you could walk around the entire thing in 20 minutes. My version of Gilligan's Island, in fact: no TV, one phone on the island, cold showers of brine water (salt and fresh water mixed together).

What a life! It was a perfect place to spend time. I got certified to scuba dive, which allowed me to explore a whole new world: swimming through clouds of fish of all sizes and colors. It was breathtaking, with stunning coral, large sharks, and barracudas. It was just amazing. Tommy, my German dive instructor, was perfect. I was his only student that week, so I got all the attention I needed. It was like having my own private instructor.

At night we often sat around on mats that were spread on the floor, as the locals played their guitars and sang. It was Fiji style, which meant lots of tuning. They drank a local drink called "Kava," which when translated into English means, "tastes like crap." It's made from a root, and leaves your mouth tasting numb.

I'd been meeting lots of people from England. I had a wonderful time diving with a married couple, Marcus and Helen, two doctors traveling back to England after working in Australia. After beating Marcus in a card game, I experienced the proper way of saying "you bastard," which sounds more like, "you bawsterd." It was so funny—a "proper" harassment, all in good fun.

In the evenings, I would often take a walk alone along the shore out to a long, narrow sand spit. There I would sit, twisting my feet into the cool sand. Eventually, I'd fall gently onto my back. Generally the wind would be blowing, intoxicating me with the pure Pacific ocean air as its sound competed against the lapping of the waves onto the beach.

Sometimes clouds raced against the nighttime sky, jumping into the illumination of the moonlight like news flashes, and eventually disappearing over the endless horizon. And when the moon wasn't there, the stars, with nothing to compete against, filled the sky with brilliance and majesty in formations sometimes familiar, sometimes unfamiliar, to my memory.

Occasionally I'd sing a prayer of joy, loud and bold enough for the heavens to hear. My heart would burst with gratitude and refuse to be caged any longer in the small box that my fear of the unfamiliar had created so long ago. Afterwards, I would wander back to my bed space, slip under the mosquito net that draped over it, and drift into dreams I'd never remember.

I extended my stay in Fiji for five days in hopes of doing some more diving, only to experience four and a half days of wind and rain. Bummer! It was during these days that I got a sense of what it must be like to be old. We had nothing we *had* to do but to entertain ourselves. We got up in the morning to have breakfast, and then sat around chatting about little things, waiting for lunchtime to arrive. Then came the long, slow afternoons, dragging along until eventually it was suppertime. After four days of this, I dreaded any thought of this being my life some day. It gave me a deeper empathy for those whose lives look this way.

The ride off the island got a little tricky as our small boat had engine troubles. We had to turn around, and the water started slipping in because the waves were so big. What fun.

Of course there were no life jackets to be found, so I spied out some empty jugs that I was planning to commandeer if we went down. "Lovely," I thought to myself, using the newfound word borrowed from my English friends. Back to the island we went. There, we waited for the tide to come back in so we could use a boat that was currently grounded. Eventually we departed once again, said goodbye to everyone again, and off over the waves we went. We came to a bridge over the river, and there they dumped us off on the bank. We stood in the rain for an hour and waited for a cab that was *supposed* to be waiting for us. (That, however, is simply reality when you operate on Fiji Time.)

Fiji Highlights:

1. Finally learning to SCUBA dive and discovering a whole new world.
2. Doing a meditation on the sand in the moonlight, only to have a crab run across Melissa's towel, causing her to scream during the calming phase.
3. The new friends from England, Finland, Germany, the U.S., Fiji, and Israel.
4. Singing at night with the locals, playing guitars and drinking Kava.
5. Cold showers, damp bedding.

I loved my stay in Fiji and Leleuvia Island. But some people arrive and never leave. Back to Nadi I went, so I could catch my plane for New Zealand, the green jewel of the Pacific.

Fiji photograph   [2], page 91   [3], page 91

Entry Four: Land of green grass

My first two weeks in New Zealand were very good. Upon landing in Auckland, I met up with some friends I'd made in Fiji. They proceeded to help me find a car that I bought for US $400. A little white Nissan Sunny! Perfect for getting me around to where I wanted to go at whatever time I wanted to be somewhere. I headed straight up north to a town named Kaeo, pronounced "Kio."

There I stayed on a farm that had been pioneered by my host family. An amazing story: it took them four months to walk to the farmstead (a distance that took me two hours to drive). Then they didn't have running water or power for years. Until 1985 they had a mile walk to the house, because no road yet existed. They were very gracious people, cattle ranchers with lots of green grass on their spread. I stayed with Margaret, and used her home as a base as I explored the area. It was like visiting my Aunt Margaret: coming home to home-cooked meals, my laundry washed and folded. Forever imprinted into my heart was the gift of waking up in the morning listening to Margaret sing. She was always singing, especially as she worked in the kitchen. My, she had such a beautiful voice!

One morning Margaret and I sat down for a cup of coffee, and chatted about various things of life. She said to me, "I want you to know my house will always be available to you, the door is never locked and most times open." As she said this, I noticed a big old country mouse scampering across the floor. He was apparently taking advantage of Margaret's open door policy. I could only smile and nod my head.

Cape Reinga is the tip-top most northern part of New Zealand. It is steeped in legend, and the jumping-off place for the native Maori people's spirits as their souls return to the sea after death. I had the place pretty much to myself, a benefit of traveling off-season in New Zealand, but I got the sense that this place was never really packed any time of year. The rolling hills and green pastures were the most lush I've ever encountered. I've never seen so many different shades of green.

Near by Margaret's was a rock called Tera Tera, an old volcanic plug. I tramped through somebody's pasture and through bush, until I finally reached the top. There I caught a breathtaking view of the surrounding valley, all the way to the Tasman Sea. I loved it, having it all to myself, no tourists, nothing but green countryside and blue water.

I got used to driving on the left-hand side as I constantly chanted, "Left, left, left, left," to myself. The people were so friendly. They say there are no strangers in New Zealand, and by the actions of most people I met, I'd say that's true.

After touching the top of New Zealand, I headed back south to Auckland to reunite with friends and make plans to continue heading south to explore more.

Here I made plans to go climbing through the Tongera Crossing, a pass through volcanic peaks and reportedly one of the best hikes in the world!

Two weeks into the New Zealand experience, I was still pinching myself and saying, "I'm really here!"

12

Entry Five: You never know...

After traveling south and saying goodbye to my traveling companions, Tamar and Tali from Israel, I prepared myself for the Tongariro Crossing: a 12-mile tramp through snow-covered volcanoes and aqua blue lakes. These are full day walks in New Zealand, and I can see why. After settling into my backpacking hostel (called Extreme Backpackers) in Turangi, I set out to the neighboring town, Taupo.

It was on the way to Taupo that I discovered I was going to need two front tires, and soon. I could see the metal threads coming through the rubber. Not a good sign. And, it was Sunday night and everything in New Zealand closes down on Sunday. I found a garage that had an after-hours number, and out came this guy dressed in nice clothes, explaining to me he had to stay clean as he changed my tire or his wife was going to kill him. Still, he graciously did it all with a smile on his face—a trait I noticed in a large number of Kiwis.

So off popped the two front tires, which practically fell apart when taken off the rim. Yikes! But after getting new tires, it was like driving a new car. I felt much better driving on wet winding roads with tires that actually had tread on them.

I arrived back at the lodge to set up for my tramping. We took off early in the morning to be dropped off at the trailhead. The walk was supposed to take about six or seven hours. The people who ran the hostel convinced me to climb Mt. Ngauruhoe in addition to the tramp, which would add about an hour on, they thought. Mt. Ngauruhoe, pronounced "nar-a-hoe-ee," is a perfectly shaped volcanic peak. It's somewhere around 8,000 ft. high and covered with snow, except where the steam vents have melted the snow away. They gave me an ice axe and crampons in case I needed them to ascend the mountainside.

When I finally reached the base of Mt. Ngauruhoe, my heart already had been working pretty hard. But I was very determined and very excited since I hadn't climbed a mountain in three years—I was way overdue. So away I went, waving good-bye to my hostel companions.

Up ahead of me was a woman also climbing the mountain, so I thought I'd try and catch up with her to have a climbing companion. I thought it would be a good idea, in case I ran into problems. As the climb continued, every time I started closing in, she pulled away. I thought, "Oh well, this will just help me to keep moving." This happened twice, and I thought that once we got to the top there would be nowhere else to go, and then I'd meet her. Eventually I did meet this person on the top. We exchanged a few words and we even took photos for each other standing on top.

At one point I turned to her and asked why she kept running away from me on the ascent. She began to share with me that she thought I was someone else, a strange man that she had met earlier and that she was trying to avoid. She apologized and said that was why she kept pulling away from me on the climb up.

She must have felt I was trustworthy, because after a couple of minutes she turned to me and said she had a strange request. She said that she'd always wanted to have her picture taken naked on top of a mountain and was wondering if I would be willing to help her out? Well, after I picked my jaw up from the ground, I said OK, giggling to myself that this woman was crazy! It was freezing out there!

But, off the clothes came except for her boots, mittens and hat. I took photos of this young Canadian girl as she held an ice axe in one hand and stood on one foot atop of Mt. Ngauruhoe. (It didn't hurt that she was good looking, either.) It was time to get down the mountain, because I had a ride waiting to pick me up. We climbed down together, chatting along the way. Eventually we said goodbye when we came to the hut where she was staying. All harmless fun; I just happened to be in the right place at the right time.

By then, though, I was running late, with the little distraction on my tramp in addition to the fact that I was a bit out of shape for climbing mountains. I was running way late, like by two and a half hours. I skeedaddled down the trail, trying to make up time. The last hour of the walk was in pitch darkness, so dark that I couldn't even see my hand in front of my face when I turned off my flashlight.

Finally I came to the car park to find Court, my ride, waiting for me. He had already taken everyone else on the trek home and then had come back to try and find me. I could tell he was pissed. He said that in another ten minutes he would have called the Rangers' office. After explaining what had happened to me, the crisis was over. I went from loser to

13

hero in his eyes in a fraction of a second! (The stuff legends are made of, as they say.) All the way home he just kept repeating over and over, "I knew I should have gone with you."

Back at the lodge in a room filled with other trampers from around the world, I stood in front of a big fire telling my story as if I had just climbed Mt. Everest, all of us rolling with laughter as I explained what had happened to me. A new travel story was born.

The walk was an incredible hike, even without the little side distraction. The weather was perfect, you could see for miles—and it was a perfect day for taking photos!

Driving down winding roads, I continued south heading for Wellington, the bottom of the North Island and the political heart of New Zealand.

A lesson from this day was clear: Keep your mind and eyes open, because you never know what's going to happen next.

You never know... photograph   [8], page 93   [9], page 93

Entry Six: SERVAS, New Zealand style

For those of you who don't know what SERVAS is, it's an organization that promotes world understanding by having members open their homes for other members who are traveling. The traveler stays a minimum of two nights, which gives some time for cultural exchange of ideas and ways of life. The host family offers free room and board and the traveler pitches in wherever he can. (My best offer is to do the dishes, given the way I cook!) I hoped for many SERVAS-host stays. It offers the opportunity to meet the real people of New Zealand; everyday people, like you and me.

I arrived in Wellington late Wednesday afternoon in time for tea, which has nothing to do with the tea you drink. "Tea time" is what they call supper or dinner. After following directions they had given me to their house, I was greeted by Anne and her six-year old daughter, Lucy. They stayed just long enough to let me into the house and say goodbye, and then ran off to pick up Mary from an after-school activity. They returned shortly and we got acquainted.

We were waiting for Brendon, the father, to return home from work when Mary proceeded to lock herself in the bathroom. Using skill and determination, she climbed out the window to her freedom, leaving us with the only bathroom in the house locked from the inside. Intrigued by the challenge, I set up a ladder to the outside window, climbed up to the windowsill, only to discover my shoulders were too wide to fit into the window. With some maneuvering, I was able to go in sideways, while perched way up on the ladder. After a bit of wiggling, I soon found myself three-fourths of the way through the window.

There was one problem, though: the windows on this old house were very high, six feet up from the floor. So the next dilemma was to figure out how to get all the way in without crashing down and smashing my face to the floor. In the small room I found a small wooden stool that I positioned for my left hand. With my right hand perched on the lid of the toilet, I slowly lowered myself into the room from a handstand! The room was now available, and I had found a new hidden circus talent.

When Brendon eventually came home, I was greeted with the question of "Who did I vote for?" After a thorough investigation, I was given the thumbs up. My stay with the family was heartwarming. I was afforded the gift of reading bedtime stories to Lucy and Mary. I also had the chance to walk to school with them and take a peek into their world. I found the children are more expressive and open here than what I've seen in the States. It was a refreshing experience and speaks well of the job the parents are doing.

Brendon was fascinated by what life was like growing up in Nebraska. I loved visiting with them, and was touched by their sincere hospitality—falling in love and saying goodbye once again.

Lucy wrote me a note that she gave me as I left, and gave instructions that I could not open it until I was on the ferry. After I had been on a ferry heading for South Island for an hour, I remembered the letter and opened it. I share it with you so you can get a taste of what I experienced. It brought a tear to my eye, in a good way. It was a homemade card, with pictures and stickers. Inside, next to two people with a large heart drawn in the middle, were these words:

Dear Dean, you'r Kind.
I like you. I will never
for-get you. you are the
second Man I have
seen with long hair.
I have a good imagination.
because, I have a world
in my imagination.
it is in my room. I like
it. the cars are cool.
p.s. I love you I hope
you have a nice Trip good Buy
good Buy good Buy
Love Lucy

Do you see what I mean? How can you not fall in love with that?

Entry Seven: Tramping, New Zealand style

After saying goodbye to my new friends in Wellington, I drove onto the car ferry, which is a huge catamaran called "The Links." After a rough ride, we landed on South Island. South Island had fewer people and more mountains. That's a good thing, in my opinion. It looked and felt a bit like Washington State and Oregon, without the people.

My first tramp was the Queen Charlotte Track: a three-day, 37-mile walk through the bush and sound, filled with stunning views of the various coves and bays. When the boat dropped me off at the trailhead, I was its only passenger. I waved goodbye to the boat captain, not realizing my desire for solitude was soon to be answered.

The first two days on the track I saw no one on the trail. Each evening I came to a backpacker (cheap lodging), but they were deserted also. When you have time alone walking in nature, you think about everything—well, at least I do. I spent 14 hours walking completely by myself. Every imaginable thought floats by: past relationships, thoughts about God, past failures and victories, concerns about future responsibilities, friends, relatives, both living and dead...everything. Strange things are remembered that only hours of quietness and silence can bring up. It was a cleansing experience, as if letting go of the past and making room for the future.

It was during this trek that I surrendered a certain aspect of this journey up to God. For weeks my mind had been screaming at me, "What are you going to do when you finish this trip?" All of my life I have been goal-oriented, planning for the next things, preparing for the advancement in life, staking out my share of the pie. But now all that I could see ahead was unclear, uncharted ground. I had no experience or benchmark to measure myself against. Each day was new and unpredictable. My mind/ego was going crazy, because there was nothing to control or move towards.

Then at a very precise spot on the Queen Charlotte Trail, I stopped. The air was fresh and heavy with moisture from the damp forest undergrowth. I waited in a still place for a length of time that seemed endless, and said out loud, "OK, I'm going to just trust... I can't see the future. I can't predict it, and I'm tired of trying to make it a certain way. Now I'm just letting that whole thing go and see where God is going to take me." At that moment a weight fell off, and from then on it just kept getting lighter and lighter. A very precious time, and a definite, marked moment of the journey.

18

My second night on the trail I shared a room with two Americans from Colorado, Hank and Janae, (pronounced "J"-nay). They were to become my new traveling companions for the next four days. It was instant friendship. Hank loved to sing all these old songs, so I would chime in whenever I could, and away we went!

Brilliant and fun, Janae and Hank added much color to my trip through the Able Tasman Track. We sea-kayaked the first day, then walked the second day on a piece of the track. We encountered golden beaches, fur seals, tons of birds, lush vegetation, clear water—oh, so nice. We spent a night on a boat in Anchorage Bay, which was more like a ship to me. The owner took us ashore to see the glowworm caves. Inside the caves, it looked like skies filled with stars on a clear night. Very cool!

When we finished our hike, a water taxi picked us up and brought us back to the starting point. It was good to have fun, easy-going tramping partners like Hank and Janae. But, like most travelers, you eventually say goodbye.

My birthday was fast approaching, and I didn't want to be traveling that day, so it was time to find a place to camp for a few days.

Tramping, New Zealand style photograph   [10], page 93

There are certain moments when being in a strange place is not so enjoyable, and so I found a home to spend my birthday. Gerard, Melanie, Nina, Lucy and Nesh were friends of my Wellington SERVAS hosts. It was there that I would plant myself long enough to be "at home."

Gerard is a freelance writer, writing mainly for *New Zealand Geographic*, and Melanie is a teacher at the local school. Kiwis are clever people, especially for creating and making do with what they have. Gerard has made a shower room entirely from stones found on the beach and a bit of glass, creating a beautiful room to shower in. They have several acres a ten-minute walk from Golden Bay.

My room was a small, single-room house out back. It was heated by a potbelly stove that burned pinecones and whatever else I could get to burn. It was bloody cold. Even in bed, I slept inside my sleeping bag. No worries though, I didn't freeze anything off. Getting out of bed in the morning, however, always took a bit of extra effort.

For my birthday I was treated to a traditional Kiwi dinner: meat and three vegetables. In honor of my birthday, I took a dip in Pu Pu Springs. The water never reaches above 52 degrees. It's supposed to be the clearest fresh water in the world. So, with a full wet suit on, and every part of my body covered that I could possibly cover, I slowly walked into the water. It was so cold that it took my breath away. Wowza! With snorkel gear on, away I went.

The colors were indescribable; that water was deceptively clear. You could see every detail, even though it was 30-40 feet deep. The vegetation was so green: watercress and stuff (I have no idea what it was) shimmered in the sunlight from above. I could see huge trout swimming around on the bottom.

This place was amazing. The amount of water that comes out of the ground per second is equal to 40 full bathtubs. So it is as if a river comes straight out of the ground. From where I swam above, I could see the dark holes with the pressure of the water shooting up, giving the same appearance as heat coming off a summer highway.

With my lips beginning to turn blue, I slipped over to another vent to view what they call dancing sands—smaller vents with piles of white sand around them, giving the appearance of the sand dancing on the bottom. An amazing sight. It was an unforgettable way to celebrate my birthday.

It was heartwarming to be a part of that special family, especially for my birthday. I will always be grateful to Lucy and Nina for teaching me the correct New Zealand way of saying "Cool!"

From there I headed down the west coast. I stopped right outside of town and picked up a hitchhiker, something I would never do back in the States. This guy was a real fascination for me. He spent part of the year fishing and the other part hunting wild pigs. Last year alone he killed 50, according to his own count.

Then he launched into his own personal protest of the DOC (Department of Conservation). He despises their use of dropping poison pellets to kill the possums. He says it not only kills the possums, but it also kills everything else as well. One day the forest is filled with life: birds singing, animals scampering around. Then they fly over and make a massive drop and a few days later there's just an eerie silence. He went on to claim that the folks in the government offices of the DOC have huge stock holdings in the companies that make the poison. I couldn't tell how much of it was true, but my first impression of the local people was that they were pretty sound. Besides, I wasn't going to argue with a guy who killed 50 wild pigs last year.

At one point I got real sleepy, so I asked him to drive. I slept like a baby for a couple of hours as we kept heading south. (Here you can do things like that!) The west coast was a long stretch of valleys, beaches, mountains, sounds, lakes, and bush. It was pure, natural beauty. The mountains have the dramatic features of the Alps, and the expansiveness of the Rockies. I was in heaven—my soul loves being in the mountains.

Using the town of Fox Glacier as my base, I spent nine hours climbing Mt. Fox. From my perch, I could see mountaintops, valleys and the Tasman Sea. It was a rugged climb through the bush. I had to climb over trees and through roots for three hours before I got above the tree line. The higher I climbed, the closer the sky kept getting, until I finally found it. With Mt. Cook as my reward, I sat viewing the highest peak in New Zealand, as a kea swooped by for a closer inspection of me. (A kea is the only true Alpine parrot.)

After the climb I drove further south, with the intention of staying on Wanaka. However, I discovered no cheap beds, so I called another SERVAS host, and away I went to Alexander. Alexander is a freezing town in the winter, covered with fog and frost-covered trees. I never saw the sun for two days.

I recouped and headed for Te Anau, my next base camp, as I explored the Southern Alps. (By the way, if you have in your mind that it's going to get warmer the further south I go, forget it. It just keeps getting colder the closer you get to the South Pole.) Te Anau was a perfect place to stay as I explored the Milford Sound and took some other treks. I climbed up Key Summit to find myself surrounded by snow-covered peaks on all sides. I left with a sense of deep peace and gratitude for the beauty before my eyes.

I explored Doubtful Sound by boat. Along the way dolphins visited us. To look into the eyes of a dolphin, to hear it speak as it swims close to the boat, left me with a sense of humility. It will forever be with me as a reminder that we share this place with others who cannot speak or protest, but still live here.

We went to a part of the sound that had ice on the surface. The top layers of the sound further back in had a layer of fresh water on top, and with the stillness and cold, they froze over. So we did a little ice breaking, a noisy affair that left me thinking that I'm glad not to be on the big icebreakers that go through the frozen seas.

With my fill of the mountains, I headed for my next SERVAS stay, a sheep farm at the bottom of South Island.

After doing a tiki tour (driving around and seeing the sights), I landed in Winton. Well, I actually landed out in the country close to Winton to stay with Stuart and Lynett McKerchar, third-generation farmers from Scotland. Here I got a real taste of Kiwi sheep farming. I helped build fences, feed animals, and learned just what it takes to be a farmer in Southern New Zealand.

I loved it. As I told Stuart, there's something rewarding about working outside, about being able to stand back and see the progress you've made, no matter how simple the task. (My task was to put wire clips on all the posts to thread the electrical wires through. Now that Wayne State College degree was really paying off!)

Their farm was 480 acres of rolling hills of grass with a few small sections of bush and trees. Almost all the farming was done on these little four-wheel motorized bikes. They did everything with them: pulled feed out to the sheep, pulled wagons loaded with fence posts, transported anything they could. You should have seen me driving around, covered in mud. I'm sure my aunt and uncle in Iowa would have been proud of me.

There were always people I met and traveled with, always sights of amazing beaches, rolling farmlands, rivers and mountains, beautiful sunrises and sunsets. Too many things to capture in words. For a brief moment, I got to see it, smell it, and taste it. All this gave me a feel for what it means to live in New Zealand.

Someone asked me on the west coast drive what the "holy grail" of my trip was. I responded that there was no holy grail, only the grail we're given each day to do with as we choose. We can either make it holy or choose not to. The choice is ours.

He took a sip of his beer, paused for a moment with a silent smile, nodded and walked away to find someone else to chat with.

South Island photographs   [11], page 94   [12], page 94

Entry Nine: Leaving time again

In Christchurch I went about town in my little white Nissan Sunny, putting up posters to sell my car. This is the tensest time for the backpacker. You have this financial investment that you hope to keep in your pocket somehow. You have a visa that will expire soon, and a plane ticket for the next destination. People who are out buying a car sense your urgency. You pray to meet the right buyer in time. Thankfully I did, and I sold the car for what I paid for it, a whopping US $400.

I thoroughly enjoyed my visit in New Zealand. The people and the beauty made it a very safe and wonderfully adventurous place to explore.

Some people sent questions to me as I traveled. (I invited anyone who had the desire to do so.) One question was this: "What was the thing I found the most strange?" That's a hard question to answer, because most things I've noticed are not "strange," but different.

Some of the differences I've noticed include no central heating in the homes (mostly electric heaters and fireplaces). Most nights you go to bed with electric blankets or a "hottie." (No, that's not a hot babe. It's a hot water bottle.) Another difference is that here folks drive on the left-hand side of the road, and they have circles you drive through at major intersections. One other thing I noticed is the friendliness of the service people. The people who pump your gas, who wait on you at tables or at the post office, store clerks and bank tellers all were curious and wanted to chat. Then there are rugby, field hockey, and net ball. (I'll leave you to look these up; I'm still trying to figure them out for myself.) Most sports you watch on TV are played by ordinary people, with regular lives and jobs, who play sports at the same time just for the love of playing the game. True sports heroes!

I left with many sweet memories, mostly of the kind people I met here and the quality in which they go about their day-to-day lives. This is a place where I could see myself living. My best stamp of approval.

My last SERVAS hosts took me to the airport to embark on the next leg of the journey. As my plane waited on the runway for takeoff, I daydreamed for a moment about coming back to New Zealand. I would renew the friendships I made there. I'd see what I missed the first time through, and then use New Zealand as the "jumping-off" point to go explore Antarctica.

I hadn't left New Zealand yet, but already missed it. Just then, as if to keep me from getting too sentimental, the plane gathered speed and took off for Australia.

Entry Ten: "Tassie" style

Tasmania is an Australian secret filled with beauty, wilderness and a rugged personality. Landing in Hobart, I jumped into a rental car and headed off straightaway to find the hidden treasures of this often-forgotten state.

Until my visit there, my basic relationship with Tasmania had been defined by the days of watching Bugs Bunny sidestep his way around the unstoppable, spinning Tasmanian devil. With my eyes keen on spotting mini-tornadoes spinning across the road, I navigated my way north on narrow, winding roads to Freycinet National Park. I spent the night sharing a large hostel with two other travelers. Ah, the beauty of off-season; in the guidebook it suggests booking two months ahead in the busy times!

I soon became aware that I was in a new place. Noisy birds called kookaburras called from the treetops. To me they sounded more like monkeys than birds. As I checked in, I looked down the porch to spy a hand reach out from a sliding glass door to feed a kangaroo. Well, a guard 'roo, I guess, instead of a guard dog.

After spending the day hiking through the bush and along deserted beaches, I continued my trip north along the coast. I stopped once to venture out onto the rocks to view a blowhole, where the waves find a way to shoot towards the sky. Powerful waves often catch people off guard and sweep them away to become fish food, so I ventured no further toward the water and journeyed on to find a place to sleep.

I drove through the countryside, and even took an old, seldom-used logging road that was suggested by someone local. Away I went, driving over rocks and through small streams, following the two dirt tracks through the grass, only to come to a hill that my car couldn't climb. Darn. So, back I went, wondering if my cheap rental car was going to be able to get back through mud holes that I thought were barely passable the first time. I discovered that speed helps. I was just glad it wasn't my own car.

Eventually I came to my SERVAS stay at a farm in a quiet little valley, owned by Alvaro and Suzanne Ascui. He was originally from Chile and she came from the States. They met when he was going to college in the States, got married, and have a whole story about living all over the place that could fill a book. It was a lovely place for me to land. Their backyard pond even had its own resident platypuses.

After spending a couple days with these two special people, I headed off to Cradle Mountain to go climbing. Along the way, I stopped at a wild game park where I was able to get up close to the real Tasmanian devil. He moved much slower than on TV. I was also able to hold a young wombat that looked like a cross between a teddy bear and a pig. He was far too cute, but way too smelly.

My climb up Cradle Mountain took seven hours of walking and scrambling over boulders covered in snow. I saw a few decent views, but mostly white and gray clouds through the snow and freezing rain. Sounds like fun, huh?

From there I headed west to the other coast, and then down, driving through the wilderness and stopping from time to time to look around. There was a moment as the sun was going down when, on my right, I caught a glimpse of a kangaroo hopping off into a field. It was one of those moments that gives you the experience of knowing you're in a different land than you've ever known.

After my time in the wilderness I found a SERVAS host in Hobart, Pam Stuart, who took great care of me as I prepared for my next adventure. Pam works for the Tasmanian Museum. While with her, I explored the history of Tasmania.

I spent a day at Port Arthur's penal colony. There, thousands of people were shipped from England in order to serve out harsh sentences of seven years or more for as little as stealing a loaf of bread. It was an interesting place, and an education on how we have treated people in the past. (America is no saint in regards to prisons, either.) It plays a big role in the history of Australia, as few people ever made it back to England. It has its role in how they think and act here, one that I find interesting.

I then caught a flight back to the mainland of Australia. The Aussie mainlanders made fun of Tasmania. They often gave me this surprised look, saying, "Why would you want to go there? I've never even been there." But I think it's one of the best-hidden jewels of Australia.

"Tassie" style photographs   [13], page 95   [14], page 95

Entry Eleven: Down Under

For several weeks in Australia, life seemed to move like molasses for me. Melbourne seemed to drag on. My bright spots were a couple of people who helped me find a car. OK, it's confession time: I'm so clueless about cars. "Put gas in, turn key, go." There's my driver's manual. So looking at car after car was driving me crazy.

I did learn a few things watching and listening to Danny as he checked over the cars I was considering. (Mostly, I discovered how much I don't know about cars.) Danny is married to the niece of Ron, my Melbourne SERVAS host. My Melbourne stay was all business around "The Great Car Search." I ended up buying the work car from Danny's friend, Trevor.

The transaction included an overnight stay with Trevor and his wife, Helen. This allowed us to drink a couple of beers and chat it up awhile—my way of doing business. Their young son kept asking me to speak English. He was fascinated by my American accent. I guess I do need a little help in this area, especially after a few Australian beers.

A good car is everything in Australia. Things are spread so far apart. It's easy to find yourself way far away from any type of town or service. Thus, my motivation to find a good car. And I did find one: a 1985 blue Ford Falcon with a V-8 engine and four doors! It was large enough to bring on passengers if I desired, and looked local enough that no one ever took notice.

So, in my 1985 Ford Falcon (a real woman-getter), off I went to explore the Great Ocean Road in Victoria. With two spare tires, extra radiator hoses, jumper cables, a large jug of oil and a large jug of water, I was as prepared as I could get. The Great Ocean Road was nice, but the real highlight was what they call the Twelve Apostles. Just imagine the Grand Canyon filled three-quarters full, its red cliffs dropping down into the blue waters of the ocean, with the appearance of going on forever and you'd then have the Twleve Apostles. Rich with history of shipwrecks, wildlife and folklore, it left a postcard memory.

From there I made my way to a coastal town that allowed me to view the most massive creatures from the ocean: whales. I watched in awe as these huge animals breached in the water, and then crashed back down into the clear blue waters.

National Geographic is great, but nothing compares to seeing it in real time, in the expanse of the endless blue ocean. Then off again to Adelaide, a town filled with churches. I went to church and then left Adelaide. After driving eight hours to get there, that was it. It was a nice town; it just didn't have much pull for me to stay longer.

Off to Kangaroo Island from there, only to drive to the ferry and discover that a round trip ticket would cost $200. Forget it. So, I started heading back east on the coast and ended up in Victor Harbor. I stopped there mainly because I saw a photo of a large dead whale in the newspaper. "Now that would be something to see," I thought. (Morbid, I know.)

I drove into town only to discover that The King still lives. A large tent was set up in their city park in that small seaside town, where Elvis was putting on a show. "Oh my God," I thought to myself, "this is where he went to!" So I peered through a crack in the tent to catch a glimpse of the man missing for so long, and sure enough, there he was, hips a-shaking and wiggling all over the place... OK, enough, but come on, I went about as far away as I could get from home and I found *Elvis*. Laughing and shaking my head, I waddled off to sign up for the penguin tour. At least they were the real things.

I love penguins. They are such a delight to watch. Maybe because it reminds me of those precious times when I went with my grandmother to the zoo to watch them in Omaha. Or perhaps it's a relief to know that there are others besides myself who sometimes look a bit awkward down at the beach. Either way, they always trigger a pleasure inside. So when I got the chance to watch large flocks of them work their way out of the rough sea, I was totally delighted. One group in particular I enjoyed: 20 of the little guys scrambled single file, as if auditioning for a Disney movie, racing for their nests. Flippers waving wildly in the air, filling the air with the little squawking noises. It was such fun. By the way, penguins smell—*real* bad—so taking one home to my grandmother wouldn't be such a good idea, even though it crossed my mind! From Victor Harbor, I headed east back through Melbourne to a place called Wilson's Prom, a national park on the ocean. This place was filled with wildlife: kangaroos, wedge-tailed eagles, wombats, as well as gorgeous, deserted beaches. The park was a place to get up close to the nature of Victoria. For those of you who don't know what Victoria is, it's a state in the southern part of Australia on the right hand side.

Look, I added that only because, before this trip, I would have had to look it up on the map—probably like the rest of you. We know so little about our cousin-country down here. I'm still trying to understand why, but it's true. They know far more about the States than I can begin to know about this place. But don't make too much of it. Most people here could tell you who the first president of the U.S. was, but they don't have the foggiest idea who their own first Prime Minister was. So we're not alone.

Driving from Melbourne to Sydney I was struck by the large pastures with an occasional, and very occasional at that, house. And this was between the two largest cities in the country. If you break down in the bush, or "outback," it's "bring-out-the-Gold-American-Express-time," or more likely, dig out all of the cash stored in all those secret hiding places—neither of which I was very excited about doing. That being said, the chances of my Falcon breaking down were minimal thanks to the expertise of my friends in Melbourne. In addition, it seemed that everyone and their grandmother in Australia knew how to fix cars, so I wasn't too worried.

I decided to head to Sydney before going inland. To give you a sense of what that meant, something like 80% of the people in this big country live on the coast. Things were about to change, once again!

Down Under photographs   [15], page 95   [16], page 96   [17], page 96

Entry Twelve: Sydney and more

I stayed with Surrey and Betty Jacobs during my two days in Sydney. Surrey is the head botanist for the Royal Botanical Gardens there. With the opportunity to chat with a real scientist in the field I once pursued, it was like taking a glimpse at a life that might have been mine.

Sydney proved to be too big for my liking. I left earlier than I'd planned, but not before I took a stroll around the famous Opera House and rode through the harbor. It truly is a beautiful city.

I definitely had my affinity for country folk, at least at this point in my journey, and their slower pace of life. So I escaped to a magic place in the Blue Mountains where I could breathe again, and take in the vast beauty there. With no other reason but luck, I landed at a brand new hostel ($6.2 million spent updating it) in the town of Katoomba, which sounds more like it should be in Africa than Australia. Wowza, it was awesome for $20 a night!

The mountains actually did have a blue tinge to the hill and valley tree-covered expanses. After hiking to the bottom of one these valleys, I opted to take a cable car ride up which was advertised as the steepest cable car ride in the world. Well, as far as my underwear was concerned, it was. Straight up the wall of this canyon we went, backwards. As we went up, my mind was constantly making plans to jump out if the cable broke, like some scene in an Indiana Jones movie. I asked them if they had a brake in case the cable broke. They said, "Yah, mate, the bottom of the canyon," and laughed. (Aussie humor.)

After Katoomba, I headed inland to get off the beaten path. I went into the real Australia, through flat and rolling pastures and deserted roadways. To a place where people still wave at you as you drive down the two-lane highway. A place where people either haven't used the Internet or really don't care, and where life is far more at ease. Driving for me is nothing new, and has given me long hours of enjoyment. So when I saw the official sign, white letters on a blue background, for a rest stop that read, "Power Nap Area," I knew I was in a good country!

Small town genuineness still thrives in rural Australia. As I headed north, I deliberately kept to the inland route. Tired of winding drives along gorgeous coastlines, I longed for the simple scenes of the countryside. I arrived in Coonabarabran.

(I'm still trying to pronounce it.) After a night of star-gazing and looking at the heavens from the local planetarium, I was off again.

I obtained a little money from the ATM and asked for directions. Someone overheard me asking and proceeded to offer his advice on where to buy gas in town. Well, there were only three stations, but nonetheless, he elaborated on how the one station was way too "dear," an expression used here for expensive. I expressed my sincere gratitude. He gave me a pat on the shoulder and said, "No worries, mate," and then walked away. I just love that.

So I took off to one of the petrol stations. Here, it's not called "gas," and when I call it "gas," all I get is the funny look and expressions that come when the mind is thinking, "Where did this clown come from?" The station also served food, so I loaded up with a true Australian brekkie (that would be "breakfast" in the Midwest). The attendant asked me if I wanted a "cuppa." I thought silently to myself, "A cuppa whata?" I nodded, just to see what might show up, and sat down. Turns out it's what they call coffee.

I really enjoyed chatting with the "inlanders" and listening to their stories. Before I left the cafe, I walked over to a couple of truckers to ask about taking some country roads. Upon finding out that I was from the States, one of them began to tell me all about the American who was friends with his father. This Yank was the person who helped start cotton in Australia (which is another story). Then with all the emphasis of the landing on the moon, he said, "He even started one of those Rotary Clubs..." There was this long pause because I was thinking there must be more information coming, like "and they discovered the cure for some disease," but, that was it. So I responded with my customary "Hmmm."

You see, all you really need to navigate through Australian language are two words or sounds: "Yah" and "Hmmm." Now, it's not as simple as it sounds because there are a dozen intonations with these two words that could end up expressing enough meaning for a word, sentence, opinion or a book. They can be used alone or several times in a row. They give the impression that you completely understand what was just said when you really don't have a bloody clue. So after giving my customary "hmmm" and nodding, I thanked him and was on my way. It's nice to be in a place where people can be that excited about a Rotary Club.

So off I went to find the country roads and forgotten stops that dot the way. I was heading north, with no plans.

Sydney and more photograph   [18], page 97

Entry Thirteen: Queensland

My drive through the back roads was a trek back in time: small towns that were vibrant, their storefronts full and alive. Angle parking, backwards, which all the women hated. Gravel and rock roads going nowhere important, with a few scattered wheat fields that offered some of the first real green I'd seen since being in Tasmania. I spent hours just driving, stopping to look at the map to see what the next town was and figuring when I'd hopefully get there. Then I drove onward after I realized that it didn't really matter because I had no plane or train to catch or appointment to make. I was just cruising. It was quiet and peaceful.

At one point I drove over Myall Creek, and by Myall Memorial Hall. They were way out in the middle of nowhere, and I thought nothing of it. Eventually I came to a small town called Lismore and settled in for the night. As bedtime approached, I picked up the book I 'd been reading called *Down Under* by Bill Bryson, and started in. (The book was so funny that many times I was caught laughing aloud in public as I sat by myself reading.)

I'd come to the place in the book where Bryson talks about Myall Creek and its historical importance, and how remote and lost the place is. It was the site of an Aboriginal massacre. And it was the first time whites were prosecuted for such a crime, and hung. This was a major change in history, since they used to hunt Aboriginal people like game animals. It just blew me away for a moment. Here I was in the middle of nowhere, with no agenda as to where to go, and bam!—I read about this lost place that I drove by, by pure accident. Well, anyway, it was a bit freaky even for me, because this is such a big and expansive place. Most likely I wouldn't have been able to find it had I wanted to on purpose. I took it as a sign that I was on the right track.

On my way north I spent a couple of days in Bryon Bay, scouting around the area. I even stumbled upon the lost town of Nimbin, a leftover 60's community stuck in time. Australians are very tolerant. As long as you don't try and project your ideas of life onto them, they give a lot of room to let people do their own thing. In Nimbin, there is a lot of "tie-die" walking around, and you can pretty much buy whatever "recreation drug" you want. (That's what they called pot.) Anyway, it was a hoot. After a fortuneteller told me that I was on an amazing journey, and that I had tamed all the demons inside, and that I was free, ("That's nice," I thought) I set off for the coast.

I continued to drive up the coast again. I loved the ocean, but it usually meant having to deal with lots of traffic (more than two cars every hour) and tourists. So I kept moving until I ended up in Murgen. What's in Murgen? Well, my friends Gina and David Temple, who I knew from my Pfizer days in the States.

Back on the farm again—and a dairy farm! Wow, I was right at home, and they provided every opportunity for me to feel that way. I was given the full tour and the freedom to walk through all the cow pies I wanted.

It was a very enjoyable stay, and for the first time in a while, a real rest. Theirs were the first familiar faces I'd seen in a while. I even spent a day raking hay. Wow, once again my aunt and uncle in Iowa would be proud of me. Just picture it: me sitting on this old John Deere, a 2040 I think, no cab, just a sun cover, in sunglasses, with miles of pastures and farm land as far as I could see; only an occasional house broke up the fields. I drove in circles for hours, and I loved it. It was a glimpse of what life is like there, the real thing. (Thankfully, I didn't break anything.)

One night the Temples had neighbors over for a "barbie." They also dairy farm. I was prompted to tell my climbing story in New Zealand, again. (It still makes me smile from the inside out, every time I tell it.) Bron and Pete Heatheringtons were important in the fact they gave me a contact in Cairnes as I continued to head north. (This turned out to be a godsend; I'll explain later.)

Feeling like it was time to go, I was on my way. It felt like I could have stayed there for weeks and worked for the pure fun of it and loved every minute. But inside there was this pull that kept me going, and staying true to that pull was what I had to do.

So saying goodbye again, away I scooted down the dirt road, arm hanging out the window, to see what lay ahead, and trusting where the winding roads would take me.

Queensland photograph   [19], page 98

Entry Fourteen: The Great Barrier Reef

Carines, pronounced like "cans," as in "cans of beer," is a tourist destination and gateway for exploring the Great Barrier Reef and Daintree Rain Forest. Arriving in Carines, I made contact with Libby, a former dairy worker for the Heatheringtons. Libby had an extra bed, so she kindly welcomed this complete stranger into her home.

This is one of the great qualities of Australia: no one is really a complete stranger. Out came the welcome beers, and the next thing I knew was I was sleeping on the living room floor, with my feet propped up on a seat of a chair, waiting for her friend Amanda to show up so I could let her in when she arrived. It wasn't until the next morning that I fully realized Amanda never made it. I never did see or speak to Amanda, so I'm not really sure if she even existed. I did learn that sleeping on a hard floor is something that should not become a habit—but beers helped.

From Libby's I drove north up to Port Douglas. I found a good hostel and proceeded to set in motion my plans to scuba around the Great Barrier Reef. Most of the people on our chartered boat went snorkeling. It was just the dive master and me who went off to explore the underwater world of the Reef that teems with life.

The clarity and multiple colors of fish were endless. They say that the Reef is dying and that in another 50 years, most of it will be gone. That's an amazing and sobering thought, considering it's the largest living thing on earth. I felt privileged to explore it, even if it was for just a day. I left hoping the predictions are wrong.

After a full day of diving I poured myself into bed early, exhausted from the long day of fun. Around 11:30 PM I woke up sensing something was wrong. I slipped on some pants and wandered over to a separate building that had a TV. It was then I discovered and watched with horror what was happening in New York.

It was September 11, 2001. In shock and disbelief, with an occasional tear, I stared at the television until 3 AM. Resigned to the fact that there was nothing I could do for those so far away, I went to bed with a prayer and a hope that it was all a bad dream.

I woke up to the reality that it wasn't a dream. In addition, I was sick. I either ate something bad or something else was going on, but food was running through me like a mighty river. I picked myself up and put my wrecked body into the car and drove north hoping to find some kind of peace in a painful day. I drove up to the Daintree Rain Forest, but truthfully, most of the day was a bit blurry. I eventually came to the conclusion that I needed familiar faces and a safe place to recover, so back to Libby's I went.

Being sick as you travel is pretty much unavoidable, but it still sucks. So Libby's apartment became my temporary hospital ward as I regrouped and made my plans to go to the "red center." I seemed to provide some kind of entertainment for Libby and her boyfriend, but I was just happy I'd found a quiet place where I could curl up and die. I mostly slept and slept, in between the frequent trips to the loo.

On a broader note, I was very deeply touched by the outpouring of sympathy expressed by the Australian people on and around 9/11. It was very common for me to hear things like, "We are keeping you and your country in our thoughts and prayers." I received several emails and calls from people I had met, and was grateful to have so many friends check in with me.

Not fully recovered but feeling anxious to get going, I commandeered two ride mates from posters I'd put up around town and headed west. Sumareta, an Irish woman, and Cathy, a Dutch girl, joined me. Off we went like one of those Disney "Amazing Adventure" stories where the lost dog, cat and hamster somehow find their way home.

I had heard about the vastness of the interior of Australia. It's a real challenge to convey in words just how much of it there is. For hours and hours we drove, through scrub and trees, and there was nothing. Occasionally we stopped at some lonesome petrol station because, after several hours of driving, if we hadn't stopped we would have run out of gas before there was even a hint of the next petrol station. We would see signs that would say, "Next available fuel, 350 Kilometers." Wowza. If you like space, Australia is a good place to be.

When there are no people, there are also no radio stations. While I was in Melbourne I was aware this would be happening, so I bought three used tapes: Supertramp, Kenny G, and a homemade version of the Indigo Girls. Needless to say, you can listen to three tapes for only so long. (Besides, Kenny G for a road trip? What was I thinking?)

So I sang, much to the disgust of my ride mates. I can never remember all the words to songs, so I just make up my own versions, even if they make no sense. Each time I started singing, my ride mates would pop their CD Walkmans on and leave me to enjoy my performance all to myself. I took it as a sign that that I shouldn't take singing up as a career. Nonetheless, away I sang, because the driver always rules.

After 2 1/2 days of driving and my singing, we pulled into Alice Springs, the main port for exploring "the great red center" of Australia. After a brief recovery from our long journey, I was off again to find the most famous rock in Australia: Ayers Rock, now called Uluru, its original Aboriginal name.

Trying to describe my experience of Uluru is a bit of a challenge. We drove for hours through the scrub desert of central Australia—hot, barren and mostly flat. Occasionally we came to a sign that declared "Flood Way." It was so hard to imagine any water in that dry, empty place that we thought such signs had to be some kind of joke being played by a roadside worker.

Eventually we popped over a hill and, off in the distance, saw this huge dome protruding into the sky. It was the remoteness that particularly made this place such a draw. In the middle of the driest continent on earth, this rock with its amazing colors and textures left me nothing but impressed.

Now, here's the downside. This place was also influenced by what I call the "Disney Effect." Load after load of tourist buses lined up to off-load all of the camera-toting-packaged-program-people like so many cattle coming down the chute. They unloaded, lined up and then loaded back up again for the next photo opportunity. There were tons of them. The crowds were hard to adjust to, much less comprehend after driving *hours* on the road and seeing so few people. Oh well, I was there in the herd, like the rest of my herd mates, clicking my camera, snapping my once-in-a-lifetime-*National-Geographic*-shot, oohing and ahhing with the pack. So what can I really say?

The other sight I visited was a place called "The Olgas," a group of amazing rock formations. They are huge skyscraper-size boulders with small green valleys cut through like cracks in a large rock. Rounded from millions of years of erosion, it reminded me of the times I walked through downtown Chicago gazing up at the unbelievable size and height of the buildings. Only this didn't have any windows or elevators—just solid red rock.

After a couple days of exploring, I went back to Alice Springs to just get away from all the tourists. I found some refuge in a place called the MacDonald Range, a string of mountains west of Alice Springs. Driving as far as I dared to in a two-wheel-drive car, I found a desert oasis in a place called Ormiston Gorge. Following a trail that led me through four hours of desert vistas that overlooked massive valleys, I was finally rewarded with a quiet that had eluded me in so many of the other places.

The trail was dry and harsh. I followed a valley that led me up to a ridge. And as I made my way I was able to experience, for a brief moment, the curiosity of all who had walked this path for the first time; the same curiosity felt for hundreds, maybe thousands of years. The curiosity of what view awaited those willing to climb this path. And for just a moment, I shared the kinship of all who had come before me, and all who will come after. Because things have been the same for so long in this old place. The common denominator was the path and the view. Everything else was just a passing glimpse. In that realization, I found a little peace.

Revived and rejuvenated, I drove back to Alice for one more day. It happened to be one of the biggest days in Alice Springs: the "Henley-on-Todd" boat races. I know what you're thinking: "But he said it was the driest continent on earth. Where is there a river?" Good question. A river *does* run through Alice. It just happens to lack water. So what they do is carry the boats through the sand in the middle of the heat as the crowd cheers them on.

I found myself in a boat, running for my life with seven others. We looked like a large centipede in 100-degree heat (with me laughing my butt off), running into the history books as we won gold for our division! The commentators were the funniest I've ever heard, with many comments not fit for this page. They were talking about a top secret U.S. military base there that no one knows about (which really does exist, because they had a boat in the race). So much for top secret.

It was also very touching to see the firefighters pass the hat around. They raised $10,000 for the families of the firefighters of New York City. This place was just about as far as you can get from New York, yet people's hearts continued to pour out to those affected back home.

With my gold medal in my bag I left Alice, going north in search of the Kimberleys, a wild and remote place on top of Australia.

The Great Barrier Reef photographs   [20], page 98   [21], page 98
                                          [22], page 99   [23], page 100

Entry Fifteen: Into the wild

Northbound from Alice Springs on the Stuart Highway, I made a stop at Bitter Thermal Springs. After hours of driving through the hot, dry heat with no air conditioning, this small oasis of green in the middle of the bush was a welcome sight. I found a small stream after a short walk. It was clear, and cooler than the air I was constantly breathing. After a quick look for crocs, I jumped in. Much to my surprise, it was deceptively deep with a strong current. I dog paddled back to shore to grab a tree root and pull myself to safety.

I was sitting there enjoying a quiet moment when an Australian family appeared, an older couple with their daughter. We got to visiting and before too long the father began to tell me about the time when he was attacked by a crocodile. The story went like this:

"I was on the piss with me mate (which means he was drinking heavily), standing on the bank of a river when all of a sudden this croc jumps up and bites me legs. I yelled to me mate, who was more pissed than I, to shoot the bugger. So he picks up his gun and shoots. But he missed and shot me in the back of me leg. (At this point in the story he pulled up his swim shorts to show me the bullet hole and the teeth marks on both legs.)

"I kept yelling at me mate, 'Shoot again, ya missed the bugger!' Eventually me mate got him."

Probably the most amazing part of this story is how funny he told the horrible event, laughing about it all the way through. He was a dairyman from Victoria, but he was unlike any dairyman I'd ever met, and I've met a few.
I stopped in Katherine for a couple of days. The heat was boiling hot. It was the "you-can't-even-touch-the-steering-wheel-of-the-car" kind of hot. So after exploring Katherine Gorge, I headed west to Kununurra, the jumping-off point in Western Australia for exploring the Kimberleys. I was signed up for a four-wheel drive exploring tour but had arrived five days early in Kununurra.

I suddenly found myself searching for ways to fill time in a small town, and I discovered a three-day trip down the Ord River. Since they wouldn't let me canoe by myself, I scrambled around and found a canoeing mate from Britain who was game for the idea, so it was all systems go. The company provided all the gear, a self-guided map and campsites. All we needed was to buy the food we wanted to eat for three days.

I love being outside in nature and was thoroughly relishing the idea of floating down a river that meanders through such a harsh place. As we shoved off from shore, I spied a crocodile swimming away and knew this was going to be an interesting trip. The water was fresh, and clean enough to drink. Daniel, my partner in all this, had only a little canoeing experience, but was totally up for the adventure that lay ahead.

By the way, fresh water crocs, which they call "freshies," are not known for being man hunters. There wasn't much to be concerned about, but I still wasn't interested in becoming the first case to find out that things had changed. So I kept my guard, and stories of poking out the eyes of the croc if you're attacked floated through my mind from time to time. (Yeah, right.)

Down the river we went with gorgeous parrots flying about, fascinating trees lining the banks of the river, and plenty of sunshine. We came around one bend in the river to discover the trees filled with bats. Big @#%$!! bats, that is, with wing spans of three to four feet. They call them flying foxes. I called them, with all of my scientific knowledge and studies, "big hairy bats."

Throughout the day we would stop somewhere along the river, jump in and cool ourselves off, or find some shade created by a cliff and soak up a cool breeze for a moment. The heat was intense, but the desire to explore never backs away from a little heat. So on we went.

Finally coming to our first campsite, we went about the chores of setting up camp and preparing for the night's dinner. While breaking up the wood for a fire, a piece of it jumped back at me and caught my leg. It was at that time that I realized I didn't have a first aid kit, so I let it bleed until it scabbed over. I've never seen wood as hard and dry as that. It burned so easily that it made me a little uneasy sleeping in the middle of the bush that was more like a tinderbox.

After pouring water over the campfire, it was time to slip into our "mozzy domes" before the mosquitoes really came out for dinner. Mozzy domes are mesh tents that allow you to sleep under the stars without getting eaten alive. There is something special about waking up in the middle of the night, opening your eyes, and having them be filled with the many lights that make up the nighttime sky.

One time I awoke, and, looking over at the campfire, I noticed it had restarted. It reminded me of something I heard a local person say once: "This place loves to burn, so be careful." Not really wanting to leave the safe haven of my mozzy dome, I laid there watching it for the next hour as it finally burned itself out.

When I sleep outside, I do something I almost never do otherwise: I get up with the sun. I learned to do this or get baked. And with that, day two began.

Off we went to explore more spectacular sights and the solace a river brings. The red cliffs dropped straight into the river, and in the right moments you could create a perfect echo. As the day wore on, Daniel began to feel the impact of the sun and was showing signs of heat exhaustion. We finally pulled into camp, and while I was gathering firewood I evaluated the situation.

The last day of the trip was supposed to be with no current because as the river approached the next dam, it became another lake. We had encountered some strong head winds, which with no current means hard work in the sun. So I ran an idea past Daniel: we do the rest of the trip that night. He was in favor of being out of the sun. As he rested, I gathered firewood to cook dinner. After eating and snuffing out the fire as dusk approached, we shoved off from shore.

I will admit it was a little risky going down a river I'd never been on before at night, but I was excited at the challenge and the unforeseen adventure. As the nighttime sky chased the light blue skies to the west and transformed it into a diamond-filled ceiling, the winds began to drop off and soon silence filled the air. Before long, there was a glow on the horizon as a three-quarters moon was in the process of showing us our way home.

The evening glowed and the water was completely still. It was like canoeing on top of a piece of glass. The canoe sliced the perfect, still surface. It felt like we were canoeing into a black-and-white photograph, as things began to lose their three-dimensional value. A sense of the surreal fell upon me. I couldn't help but smile. Occasionally as I looked up into the nighttime sky, I could make out the silhouetted outline of large bats flying overhead; our black navigators were watching over us.

As we approached home, a motorboat went zooming by us. I flashed my torch a few times so he could see us. All I could hear coming from the boat was, "It's a bloody canoe! They should have been back hours ago, crazy buggers!" I just laughed.

Four hours later, we pulled into our home port. After a 40-minute walk to my hostel, I hopped into my car to go get Daniel and our gear. Tired, but feeling pretty good, we slipped back into the hostel and fell fast asleep.

Into the wild photograph   [24], page 101

Entry Sixteen: End of OZ

The Kimberleys are a vast area of wilderness. They are so vast that at one point during WWII, the Allies were going to let the Japanese have it just to see if they could survive there. One could spend a lifetime exploring this place and never see everything there is to see—and probably never see people again.

Early one morning I loaded up into a four-wheel-drive vehicle with three other paying tour members to go explore a small piece of this open land. For hours we traveled down a dusty dirt road. Occasionally the guide would point out some wildlife along the roadside. But mostly I spent the trip suspended in midair between the roof and the seat. We came upon a river that covered the road and had signs posted: "No Swimming," and a picture of a crocodile on them. Unless the crocs could jump up and open the door, we were safe from harm as we drove through the river.

When you're stuck in a small area for hours with people, you get to know about them whether you want to or not. My companions included an Aussie woman called Sam, a pomie (nickname for someone British) called Samone and an Italian called Roberto, whose nickname was Ferrari (why, I have no idea). Eventually we came into a deserted campsite next to a river, and set up camp for the night.

We all had swags, which is a contraption invented in Australia. It is a canvas-covered sleeping bag that has a little extra padding for the hard ground you lay it over. It's supposed to be snake-proof, except for the portion where your head pokes out. Generally I slept on top of it and covered myself with a sarong that I had bought in Fiji.

We found a water hole in the river where a small waterfall filled a rock-formed pool. The water was refreshing after our long ride, and served as our bath for the day. Later that night, after dinner was long over, I sneaked back to this place and went for a dip in the light of the full moon. It was as peaceful as one could imagine, with the white light of the moon splashing across the water. We were far from everywhere, and that was what I wanted to feel, for a brief while anyway: to be far from everywhere. No matter what else was happening in the rest of the world, in that moment it was all far from where I was, and I was peaceful. For that I will be ever grateful.

Waking with the sun once again, we had a quick brekkie and were off to explore more wilderness. Our guide Justin also brought Kim, a mate of his. Kim was a cowboy who had spent many years mustering cattle at various stations across the outback. Kim provided a great deal of entertainment throughout the trip in the form of stories that kept the women generally in a state of fear, and the rest of us wondering if the stories were really true.

After another day of exploring waterholes and views of wildlife, we came to our base camp for the next three nights. From here we explored the upper part of the Kimberleys. This was a majestic place called Mitchell Falls, named after the person who was governor of Western Australia at the time. Mitchell Falls is a four-cataract waterfall that eventually plunges into the Indian Ocean.

This region is one of the most isolated and stunning sights in the Kimberelys. Full of Aboriginal lore and art work, it offered a great place to explore and discover what few have experienced. We spent our time hiking throughout the area and jumping in the river occasionally to find a little relief from the scorching heat. We explored the gorges cut by the river in the wet season. During the season I was there, the gorge was mostly dry and full of smooth rock that showed the signs of relentless and powerful water that had pounded it into a burnished submission. Soon water would be polishing the gorges again with the return of the wet season, but for now, it was available for us to explore.

One afternoon we followed a river upstream and found a mini-gorge where we decided to camp out for a short while. Kim fished for our lunch as we explored the amazing waterhole and slept in the cool shade made from an overhanging ledge. They cooked the fish by laying them on the embers of the small fire. Justin went on to explain that this was probably not so different from how the Aborigines would have spent the day. All I was sure of was the fish tasted amazing with the charcoal flavor of the fire. And the shade was perfect—no flies.

On our many Australian side trips, I became very intimate with a grass called "spinafix." Each blade of grass ends in a needle-sharp point that distributes a resin that causes an itching and stinging sensation. It pretty much sucked, but was part of the price to pay to go exploring. Another interesting surprise was the green ants. They possessed an amazing ability to turn a reasonable person into a complete madman as they bit you endlessly. We all took our turn at this interesting display of a dance as we jumped around trying to get them off our bodies.

Each night we would eventually return to camp, exhausted in a good way from the day of exploring. It occurred to me that people these days want the thrill of the journey; they want the growth and rush that comes from the adventure. But they want this without really being willing to pay the price that is required from those who dare. That's why the Disneys and the Las Vegases of the world leave you a bit empty when you're finished. They don't bite anything but your pocketbook, and do little to stir the soul. I became a bit thankful for little green ants that bite.

Somehow in the evening I started telling bedtime stories to my camp mates. This was usually after a sip or two of a nightcap, but that's how some things happen. I think I'll write a children's book about it, titled "The Search for the Holy Wallaby." Each night was a continuation of the search for the Holy Wallaby that in some humorous way captured our day. It started like this: "Once upon a time there were four travelers. They came from the Kingdoms of Italia, Britainia, Australia and Americania. They all were in search of the Holy Wallaby because the Holy Wallaby had every answer to every question that could ever be asked...."

And if you want to hear the rest, you'll have to wait for the book.

My last two weeks were spent in Darwin, in preparation for my next leg of the journey in Asia. I sold the Blue Mean Machine I had been driving around to a couple of young German backpackers who had just landed and were about to do the reverse of my route. It's always a great relief to get your car sold because of the chunk of money involved.

While in Darwin I acquired some new friends: Jolanda from Holland, who taught me a few words of Dutch, and Itamar from Israel, who had this ability to make me laugh. We had several water volleyball matches that involved almost every country in the world, and played for the championship of the universe many times. I was sad to see them leave, but that's what travel does: it gives you a brief moment to share life and then say goodbye.

I extended my stay in Australia after getting sick, not wanting to set off into Bali as an invalid. It worked, so I was well and rested for the unknown.

After 16,000 kilometers I said goodbye to Australia. It was a long-awaited, almost forgotten dream to come to this place that once felt so far away. I took with me a small sense of what it means to be an Australian. The people are generous with those they meet, and are far more related to Americans than I'd imagined. They are like cousins whom we don't get to see often, but are always so happy to see when we reunite.

I would love to return to the land of OZ and see more hidden treasures of the place "Down Under." It no longer seems so far away. All I'll ever have to do is find the place in my heart where I keep the friendships and personal treasures that I found in Australia, and that will take me back.

Saying goodbye to Australia was like saying goodbye to family. It also was the last western country I would be in for a while. My next jump to Indonesia would be my first encounter with a third-world country.

I did have some concerns about going to Indonesia. There were reports coming out of Indonesia about gangs roaming through the cities "sweeping," a term used to indicate their policy of removing all westerners because of the U.S. war being waged in Afghanistan against the Taliban. Indonesia is 80% Islamic.

It was hard to get accurate information about what was really happening in Indonesia; all the news was bad news. At one of my doctor appointments while I was ill, I talked with the doctor about my concern. He said, "Go; you'll be fine. It will just be a different experience." He had grown up in Africa and witnessed many challenging experiences.

I decided to trust his advice and not let fear dictate where I went or what I did. Using my head and trusting my heart, away I went to discover Indonesia.

End of OZ photographs   [25], page 102   [26], page 102   [27], page 102
                              [28], page 102   [29], page 103

Entry Seventeen: From West to East

Departing Darwin, I left behind the familiar things, and even those that weren't so familiar (like driving on the left-hand side of the road). My driving days would not resume for some time.

I landed in Denpasar, Bali, and headed straight towards Ubud, which is the cultural heart of this exotic island.

In Bali, everything is negotiated. I asked for a taxi and got a quote for 50,000 rupees. I offered 25,000. The driver responded, "No, it costs much more than that." I said, "Fine, I'll find another taxi." He replied, "OK, OK! Let's go."

That is the process used for almost every transaction there. Everything is bargained for, or you end up paying too much. The only time I don't try negotiating is when I have to go to the bathroom so badly that I'm willing to pay almost anything. I'm just happy to have a clean toilet.

On my ride to Ubud I met a British couple. Cat was a doctor and Jon was a professional mountain bike tour guide. We were soon sharing a taxi in our search for a room. After some searching, we found a home to stay in. The cost was 45,000 rupees per night, which is US $4.50 a night—and that included breakfast.

I had been told that Southeast Asia would be much cheaper than many parts of the world. It was, almost embarrassingly so. You haggle over $1 like it's $100. It's a part of the culture to negotiate, and you win respect if you bargain hard. One thing though: it took time, which I usually had. We spent a great deal of time walking around, looking at things, visiting with people.

There were endless temples on Bali. The religion is mainly Hindu, with a pinch of local religion mixed in. It was moving each morning to see the offerings of the local people. They set out small piles of rice on a green leaf with a flower as an offering to their ancestral spirits. They did it all gracefully and with deep respect; it was as natural as eating for them. While I was in Ubud, a festival was going on. This particular festival happened every six months. So, with a little shopping I adorned myself in a traditional Balinese outfit. This consisted of a white shirt, two sarongs (with the yellow one on top) and a white padang, which looks like a bandanna, tied around the top of my head. No matter how hard I tried, I still didn't look Balinese with my white skin and my nose. But the locals appreciated my efforts. The outfit even allowed me to enter a sacred temple, normally closed off to visitors, for the festival.

Inside the temple was an amazing array of yellows and reds surrounding various altars, with holy men chanting prayers in high places. The temple was alive with ceremonial dancing and music. The smell of incense filled the air.

I wandered toward the back of the temple and found myself in the middle of the prayer service. After watching for a while, I ended up sitting on the ground with the rest of the people as the Holy Man rang his bell and chanted his prayers. I didn't have to be Hindu or understand Indonesian to appreciate the love and devotion these people carried in their hearts; it showed in their eyes and was sent with their smiles. It filled the air, like the rising moon over the thatched roofs.

As I sat there, a woman sitting next to me smiled and gently pushed over a bowl filled with flowers and a burning incense stick. The flowers are put into your hands as you put them together in prayer, as part of the offering and prayer; a beautiful act in itself. The incense smoke is used to purify your hands each time you say a prayer. I was prepared as much as I could be, and I followed everyone else's lead as best I could. It was very touching, and for a brief moment I was granted the gift of joining in the experience of worship and devotion with these beautiful people. It ended with a special blessing for each worshiper from the Holy Man.

Later on I was sharing with my home-stay host how much I appreciated the experience, and he responded to me in his limited, broken English, "Maybe we pray to same High God even though you Christian and me Hindu." Some would argue this not to be true; my heart knows differently. And maybe a little hope is nurtured for a future where we can all live in one world.

Speaking of beautiful, the women in Bali are amazingly beautiful. It's just too bad that they don't speak much English. I tried not to stare, but sometimes the only thing that saved me were my sunglasses.

Tourism was down in Indonesia, as it probably was almost everywhere in the world at the time of my journey. In addition, Indonesia has had a number of demonstrations, a topic I'll save for another time. At a time when the streets and stalls would have normally been filled with shopping tourists, Bali at times felt completely deserted. Even though Bali felt a bit touristy, it seemed to have hung onto its customs and traditional way of life.

Bali made me aware that a new part of the journey had begun. People no longer spoke English as a first language. Bali also was a turning point for how I felt about the trip. For the first two months it really felt like I was on a vacation, even though I knew I wasn't. But during that time in Bali, there was this nagging feeling that my journey was moving too fast, and it was going to be over before I wanted it to be. "How could that be," I asked myself, "I don't even know how long I will be traveling?"

The vacation feeling lasted until I left Australia. In Bali, it transitioned into something new. I started to discover a new place within me that could be uncovered only on a long journey, where time begins to take on different dimensions and days melt together like scoops of ice cream on a hot day. There was still a small element of urgency, but it no longer seemed to have the control it once did. And with that shift, I began exploring Indonesia, a surprise stop on my trek.

From West to East photographs   [30], page 104   [31], page 105

Entry Eighteen: Dragons and more

While in Ubud, I met a young Israeli woman named Neta. It was Neta's dream to see the Komodo dragon.

Since Komodo and Flores Island kept popping up on my radar screen, I decided to team up with Neta and pose as her boyfriend. Two important points to understand: one, a woman traveling by herself gets treated very differently than one traveling with her partner; and two, for the most part it's illegal for Israelis to enter Indonesia unless they jump through many political hoops. It's an Islam versus Jewish thing. So the next leg began with Neta posing as either an Italian or someone from Malta, with me (almost 20 years older than she) as her boyfriend.

After an all-night ferry ride and a minibus ride across Sumbawa Island, we arrived to find the ferry there wasn't leaving at 8 AM, but at 4 PM. In addition, it no longer stopped at Komodo Island. So, with a Swedish couple we'd met on the ferry, we hired our own boat. As if from right out of a picture book, we popped onto this boat that reminded me of the boat in the movie *The African Queen*, with Humphrey Bogart and Katherine Hepburn. (If you don't know about it, rent the movie.) Not one member of the crew spoke a word of English. Thankfully I had a phrase book, but it was limited to very basic conversation, like, "Where's the toilet?"

Off we sailed, with the "putt, putt, putt" sound of the engine in a boat that was handmade and looked to me to be tied together with baling twine. We leaned against our backpacks under a blue tarp on the small wooden deck as our boat crossed clear blue water, under clear blue sky.

After motoring for three hours we pulled into the bay of a small island. We had no idea as to why we were there, or even where we were. The Swedish couple was convinced the crew was going to kill us and take our belongings. Neta drew a map of the boat and an arrow to the island. This somehow got interpreted as a sign we wanted to go to shore. So with everyone else claiming "no chance" of leaving the boat, I crawled into a handmade dugout canoe. I put my exploration hat on and said a little prayer as the others took a photo of me paddling toward shore. I got to shore, walked around for ten minutes, then climbed back into the canoe and paddled to the boat.

Like some great explorer, I brought back treasures (seashells) to my traveling companions and laughed. Because *I* think they pulled into this beautiful bay to offer us a rest and let us swim. The "going to shore" idea got started by Neta's map.

So I jumped into the clear blue water to take a dip, which seemed to make the crew happy. Someone was finally going for a swim.

We continued to head east, passing through currents the likes of which I'd never seen before. Like rivers in the middle of the ocean, they ran over hidden bottoms and created upswells and whirlpools strong enough to swallow a canoe. Occasionally the crew would unfold a small, torn sail made of empty rice bags sewn together at the front of the boat. Putt, putt, putt, on we continued. After seven hours, we asked how much more of the five-hour trip there was. We were told we had three more hours.

Well, there wasn't much to do but enjoy the ride. I was loving it, anyway, and to me it didn't matter. Here we were on this authentic Indonesian boat, traversing through some of the most dangerous water in all of Indonesia. It was definitely a *National Geographic* scene. Eventually the sun went down and the nighttime sky filled itself once again with those diamonds on black velvet. With the tarp rolled up, we laid on the deck staring at the stars as we wound our way through darkness.

It was one of those magic moments of knowing there was no place I would rather be than right there on my back watching falling stars jet across the nighttime sky. I found myself wishing it would never end, even with the occasional "lungs-filled-with-engine-fumes-moments." But it did. Eleven hours after we started, we pulled into Komodo Island, our home for the next two nights. We were more than ready for a toilet that was more than just a hole on the floor of the boat.

Komodo Island is a national park, but we were the only visitors spending the night. Since the ferry stopped coming to Komodo, visitors had stopped coming. We were offered the staff's full attention and became their entertainment, to some extent. There's no TV or radio on Komodo, so things got a bit slow with no tourists.

I have to admit I didn't really know anything about the Komodo dragon (probably much to the disgust of my Wayne State biology teachers) except some vague memory of a *National Geographic* special. But I can tell you this, once you've seen one, you gain an entirely new appreciation for this large creature found nowhere else in the world. Creating a scene not so different from *Jurassic Park*, these large lizards meandered around the island in search of food and water. The larger ones were as big, if not bigger, than I was. With their slimy mouths waiting to chomp on their next dinner, I made sure I kept my distance—or at least made sure I was with someone who was a slower runner than I. Neta was in heaven.

After two days, onward we went with four more passengers: park staff who were stranded on the island. We were happy to have someone along to translate. We stopped at a fishing village, which gave us a chance to explore a quieter kind of life. Small children called, "Hello mister," as I strolled among the thatched houses. For those who had so little, they were generous with those they met.

Neta continued to be referenced as looking like the Mother Mary, which seemed to bring them (and her) much pleasure. We landed in Labuanbajo, Flores Island, in the late afternoon and said goodbye to our new friends to find a room. This was a pattern that kept repeating itself.

I was told Labuanbajo had world-class diving, so I went to find out for myself. And yes, it's true: it does have world-class diving (as if I would really know— I've been on a dive only ten times). I did two dives there. Both were incredible. I once again explored a fascinating underwater world, filled with fish of every size and shape imaginable.

On the second dive I was fortunate to have a meeting with a manta ray. This was totally magic. This creature was huge, but floated through the water so gracefully, and with what looked like no effort. I just sat there in awe. My dive instructor was in spasms of joy over the encounter. People spend an entire dive season hoping to catch a glimpse of one of these amazing creatures and I saw it in the only dive I allowed myself there. I'm a lucky man.

Labuanbajo was the starting point of our exploration of Flores Island. From there we traveled the island, stopping at various small villages and towns to explore surrounding countryside and the culture of these small communities. Flores is a large, rugged and stunning island. Full of amazing valleys and dominated by a string of volcanoes, the difficult terrain has divided many of the villages into distinct ethnic groups. This has had both a positive and negative effect. The positive is the beauty of such a remarkable place and the preservation of local culture and customs. Negatively, it takes forever to go short distances, as the road winds around like a snake, following the unending ridges.
This was no place for those who get carsick. I found myself remembering an old school fight cheer: "Lean to the left, lean to the right, stand up, sit down, fight fight fight!" Take that and multiply it by four to eight hours, and you have a typical bus ride. Add that to the once-a-day flat tire ritual, and you begin to get the picture.

Flores is off the beaten tourist path, a fact that I relished. This changes how people respond to tourists. People become curious again. They come forward to find out who you are and why you're here. One might have thought we were celebrities, as a crowd would follow us around to just listen. It was heartwarming, and a little annoying at times, because they never wanted to stop.

I was very aware of the impact my visit might have, so I took it on myself to be a one-man ambassador for the U.S., since this was what I really was. I wanted people to be left with a positive impression of the U.S. so when they read stories that may say differently, they have a memory of something else. And maybe that moment of kindness will carry over into the judgments we all form.

In the U.S., we leave it to our government to create relationships with other countries. But many times I personally feel my own government doesn't always represent the average "American Joe." For sure, the American government doesn't know how to connect with the average "Indonesian Joe." If we want the responsibility of being a world power, then we should be responsible to know and understand who the world is. We should know them not by what our government and media say alone, but for ourselves and in our own personal relationships. As we do this, we might begin to see that the world isn't always the way our media and government portray it. It is then that we can begin to take real responsibility for creating a world that can live together.

All right, off the soapbox. But every now and then a few words to make us think does the soul good. Back to Flores.

One of the small towns we visited was Bajawa, nestled in the middle of a green valley surrounded by volcanic ridges. It was a small gray spot in a vast sea of green. While there, we embarked upon a village tour that took us to the countryside and further off the beaten path. The last tour our guide led had been two months before, so we were a bit of a novelty. He took us to his home village, about one-half hour from Bajawa, and into his mother's house. There he explained many traditional customs and answered our questions.

In the kitchen, which was basically an open fire pit in the corner of a room, several chicken feathers were stuck on the wall. I asked the guide what the significance of this was. He asked his mother and as he translated, she gave this explanation: "Each time we kill a chicken, we look at the chicken's heart. By looking at the chicken's heart, you can determine if your children are going to have good or bad luck." She was still practicing animist rituals, a first for me, which I found fascinating. All of the villages we visited still practiced animist rituals, which connected with events ranging from births, marriages, and deaths, to the building of a new house.

After the tour of the villages, we stopped back at the guide's home village for a moment. While waiting for him, I popped out of the car and jumped into a volleyball game that was being played by the villagers. This was a big hit. With no English-speaking team members, I rambled around the court and hammed it up. It brought me great joy to be able to connect with them for a brief moment and have us all laughing together.

The day ended with a trip to enjoy some hot springs. I always thought such sites were just outside of town the way they talked about them. But an hour later we made it to the hot springs. I was stoked; my first hot bath or shower in a month! The springs were amazing. They brought back memories of New Zealand, except this water was hot instead of bone-chilling. So, we took our baths with about 30 other locals, who seemed more interested in us than taking their baths. I didn't care; I was just happy to have plenty of hot water.

The next major destination was Keli Mutu National Park. Packed on a bus once again, we wound down the road surrounded by amazing waterfalls and plush green valleys. I was anxious to get a better view, but I was stuck standing in an overcrowded bus. So I climbed out the door (with the music of Indiana Jones playing in my head) and up onto the roof of the bus as it was running down the crooked road.

The four young men already riding on top met this with much delight. They were kind enough to make sure I got the best seat up front. I hung on to anything that I could find bolted down to the roof. With the wind blowing across my face, I soaked up the amazing views: terraced rice fields, majestic, cascading waterfalls and treetops filled with monkeys.

It was all going well until the rain came. When the rain comes in Flores, it really pours. The boys gave some kind of shrieks that must have translated into "STOP NOW, HURRY," and we scrambled over the top of the bus and squeezed back in. Well, *mostly* back in; half of me was still hanging outside because the bus was way too crowded. So with half of me completely soaked, we pulled into Moni and found a cafe where we could eat and wait out the rest of the storm.

We found a gem of a home to stay in. The owner, Marie, cooked these amazing dinners for us each night. In addition, the first night's meal was completely prepared over an open fire, because the power went out.

Kele Mutu is the home of three colored volcanic lakes. They are one of the most amazing things to see in the region. They continue to change colors, an event that is completely unpredictable and unexplainable. At 3:45 AM, a knock on the door greeted us to pull our sleepy bodies out of bed and venture out into the pitch dark.

Trusting this was really worth seeing (given it's even drawn on the back of the 5,000 rupee note), I wandered with eyes half-open and climbed into the small bus. Neta never said much in the morning except for a few grunts, so the ride up the mountain was pretty quiet. The minibus was packed with every tourist in town, all nine of us. Five Swedes joined us. Once we reached the base of the mountain, up the trail we marched in a race against the darkness, trying to get to the top to see the sunrise. We won.

The lakes were amazing: grand in size and black, turquoise, and a light chocolate brown in color, like something from Willy Wonka's chocolate factory. We spent the morning wandering around the rim of the craters, watching the bubbles in the lake far below. It was quiet there, the kind of quiet you get when you're in the mountains alone. I loved it, and it was a reminder to me just how much I love climbing mountains. In the warm sunlight, surrounded by cool air, I found a comfortable place on the ground and took the kind of nap where both body and spirit rest.

The evenings in Moni were special. Generally the power would go out in the small town leaving only kerosene lamps and candles to light rooms. At one point I was standing outside gazing at the stars; the Milky Way never looked so bright. I looked up a nearby hillside and saw a tree that appeared to have a fire underneath it; the light was flickering off the leaves. I studied it for awhile, and became curious when I couldn't see any fire to produce the light. Pulling out my small binoculars, I discovered the tree was filled with fireflies. Looking through the lenses, it was as if I was watching a tree filled with thousands of stars. It was so beautiful, and so quiet.

Do you know what people do when there is no TV or radio to play? They talk to each other. Each night I was afforded the privilege of watching Marie put her four children to bed, and each night I got to feel the warmth a mother has for her children. After some conversation about the day, Marie would begin to sing them to sleep. Every now and then a child's voice would blurt out something as Marie continued to just sing, softly and sweetly, to her children until there were no more blurting questions. There was just silence and a dark candlelit room. I was thankful for thatched walls that allowed voices to pass through.

We left Moni and arrived in Muamerri where I said goodbye to Neta, my brave little travel mate. Onto the plane she climbed, but I wasn't alone, because we had met a young Indonesian man named Nando. Nando and I were to become traveling companions. Lucky me.

Nando was an amazing young man, far more worldly and mature than most 25-year-olds I've met and known. He had a wonderful sense of humor and an ability to connect with everyone he met. We traveled together for the next four days, meeting local people and discussing life in general. What also made Nando special was his level of English. It was the first time I'd found someone from Indonesia with whom I could share discussions of complex issues. It gave me a chance to really find some deeper understanding of Indonesia. He was always addressing me as "Mr. Dean," and in return I called him "Mr. Nando."

He shared with me many stories, like how he got his name: "When I was born my father was listening to the radio and the ABBA song *Fernando* came on. The rest is history."

Even though Nando had never been out of Indonesia, he knew and understood more about the world than even myself. Neta had been impressed because he even knew of the different tribes in Israel. He had an insatiable hunger to know and understand. He shared about the struggles of his country, about the demonstrations he had participated in. He told how he had spent a month in jail for burning a homemade paper version of the American flag at an anti-capitalism rally. He told us how his cousin had been killed by a stray bullet as the military mowed down protesters in his hometown.

We were able to have frank discussions out of a deep respect for each other's opinions and experiences. He asked good questions like, "What can you do when the military backs large businesses, who receive kickbacks all in the guise of capitalism, in order to keep in line those who barley eke out a living? What do you do when those who attempt to organize some level of power and dignity for ordinary people often go missing? Do the people in the U.S. understand or even care that the shirt they just bought was produced by someone working ten hours a day, seven days a week, for only two-hundred dollars a month?"

His questions weren't an attack—they were a search to look into the soul of the American people and see if they had any understanding of the impact they have on the world. "We don't ask for much, just a better life," Nando told me. I asked him what a better life meant to him. He paused for a moment to think and then responded, "A chance to acquire an education and the opportunity to receive some healthcare."

He was right; they weren't asking for much. He didn't want handouts, just opportunities for basic human dignity. The best I could offer was to listen and learn for myself firsthand.

Nando watched over me like a mother hen as we ferried our way to West Timor. The ferry from Flores to Bali was dry-docked for a week, so I either could wait a week or continue on with Nando. Since traveling with Nando was far more interesting than hanging around Maumere, on we went. It was like having my own personal guide and translator as we explored new places together. Nando told me about the land from where he came, a remote place called Irian Jaya. He spoke with passion and reverence of the mountains that possessed what he called "everlasting snow." I promised that someday I would come back to explore his land. When I told him that together we'd find the mountains of everlasting snow in one of the last truly unexplored areas of the world, he smiled.

Kupang, West Timor was a short visit, nothing remarkable, just very good company. Onto the fast ferry I climbed, waving goodbye to my new friend. I was sad to be leaving him, yet happy to be traveling alone again. There was this understanding within me that this was a solo journey, with many partners and teachers set along my path to take me to every imaginable place inside me.

And so, north I went.

Entry Nineteen: Leaving Indo

While in Indonesia, I came to the discovery that I was on a pilgrimage. God had known it all along and was just waiting for me to catch on.

While in Yogakarta, Java, a friend introduced me to a book entitled *The Art of Pilgrimage* by Phil Cousineau. I won't bore you with the details, but I must share with you that as he described the preparation and actual experience of a pilgrimage, it matched almost exactly what I had instinctively been going through. It was a clarifying point on my journey, one that brought into greater focus the mystery that continues to unfold before my eyes. With this deeper understanding, my journey continued.

Since the beginning of my journey I'd felt within my soul that it was impossible *not* to embark on this adventure, and to do so would be like trying to ignore the very essence of my life. It's difficult to articulate and impossible to explain, yet each place to which I ventured had a treasure or jewel to offer. I, in return, offered myself. It was my responsibility to accept the treasure graciously, and to present something sacred in return.

One of the greatest discoveries I made on the journey was finding the presence of the sacred wherever I went, especially in the simple things. While riding a becak (bicycle-rickshaw) in Yoga, traffic was jammed and moving very slowly. Typically, many small mopeds filled the streets carrying everything from a four-person family to tied-up goats. In front of me, a small child was sandwiched between her mother and father. Smiling, I reached out slowly to shake her hand. The child took my hand, closed her eyes, bowed her head and touched her forehead with the back of my hand. She smiled and turned back to her mother. I don't know the cultural meaning behind this gesture, but I knew the feeling of respect when it was offered, and I knew the feeling of grace when it was presented to me. For a moment I felt like a king or holy man being greeted. And for a moment, I was.

As I moved from one place to the next, I generally took the cheapest possible way without compromising too much safety. I tended to steer away from night buses; it was pretty hard to see much of the countryside at night. Still, one evening I decided I needed to make up a little lost travel time by taking a night bus. After some intense negotiating, I obtained a ticket for Yogakarta. The trip lasted ten hours. We took intermittent stops so the driver and the rest of us could eat because during Ramadan, they don't eat during daylight hours.

The bus was only half full and as I boarded, I commandeered the back seat all to myself thinking I had "won the prize." Well, it turned out to be a prize all right: the booby prize! All night long there was a slow drip from the air conditioner that roared above my head. Too tired and lazy to move, I just kept shifting in the seat hoping to find a dry and safe place. Each time I moved the cold drip seem to follow me, like a magnet to metal, hitting me somewhere on the face just as I was about to fall back to sleep. The final straw was when the bus hit some type of large bump in the road and my body went airborne before finally coming to rest on the floor of the bus. At that point I surrendered and found a new seat.

In Yogakarta, a local man named Sindhu and his Australian friend Cynthia befriended me. Cynthia was a two-time New Zealand surf champion who had been coming to Indonesia for years. And Sindhu was a local hero who was once one of the most wanted men in Indonesia due to his participation in demonstrations against the government. Meeting them transformed my week; it opened doors into local homes and to secret places often missed by passers-by.

One of the places they took me to was an old underground mosque that once was used to hide people during the Dutch occupation. The acoustics there were amazing. On my final night in Yoga, I wandered back there to sit alone for a peaceful moment. The most amazing song that I had never heard before came out of me; it was a song of prayer. I only wish I had recorded it. But it was meant for that moment only.

One evening, Cynthia went to a healer to have him work on a back problem that had been bothering her for years. I was invited to come along and watch. While Parentio worked on Cynthia, we had a discussion about life, God and my journey. It was a mystic conversation, shared as I sat on the floor of his humble home made from a section of a crumbling old building that had been part of the Sultan's water tower years before.

Sindhu was translating for me when needed as we dove into the sacred issues generally avoided in conversation. At the end of the evening, some four hours later, he indicated he had something for me. He walked into another room and came back with a traditional shadow puppet, a white monkey. This monkey symbolized wisdom, truth, leadership, honor and the connection to God. He said, "Many people have asked me for this puppet and I've always said no, because it belongs to someone special. I've been waiting for nine years for that person, who is you." With a quiet reverence I accepted his gift, a symbol with deep meaning for both of us.

Back in my room I placed the puppet next to the old Kris (ceremonial knife) I had acquired earlier. It was as if they were meant to be together. The Kris, which was supposed to be over 300 years old, was said to be endowed with the supernatural powers of the ancestors. Both became a part of my own sacred altar when I returned home.

Next to Yogakarta is Borobudur, the largest Buddhist monument in the world. Built around 750-850 AD, it was mainly forgotten until rediscovered around 1815. Imagine the pyramids of Egypt carved into an ornate altarpiece, then you'd have Borobudur. I hired a guide who explained the stone carvings and panels of the terraced temple. After the tour, we parted and I headed back to embark on my own personal prayer walk.

I followed in the footsteps of those who'd walked before me over 2,000 years ago, in search of what secrets Buddha might reveal to me. In silence, with the rain falling, I walked for two hours, up terrace by terrace until I finally reached the top. Feeling as if I was transported back through time, I sensed the presence of those so devoted, and the peace found by those who searched. The rain continued to fall, and so did the walls around my heart.

Saying goodbye to my new family—which all those in Yogakarta claimed to be—I headed north again to Jakarta. There I spent only a night, because if there would be any trouble in Indonesia, that would be the place. It is the heart of all the demonstrations and the hub for all the political scenes. The energy on the streets seemed electrified by an unsafe feeling.

With no real reason to stay, I flew to Medan en route to Bukit Lawang, home of the orangutan rehab center. Bukit gave me the chance to get into the jungle and see firsthand the wild parts of Sumatra: trees filled with things that crawl, climb, bite and suck. Doesn't that sound exciting? One afternoon I awoke from a nap to find a huge spot of blood on the sheets of my bed. I discovered a leech had attached itself to my ankle and then fallen off as I napped after hiking in the jungle. Nature can be both beautiful and nasty: hikers beware.

I spent my last days in Indonesia talking with people, and just walking around a city that seemed to be filled with curious people. I never once had any problems, even though I was told not to go walking. As a matter of fact, many local people commented that it was better that I was there than in America: "It's safer." Which made me wonder: does anyone back in the States realize that many people are afraid to come to the U.S. because they think it's dangerous? So the next time you hear about a place not being safe, remember much of what is written is a tiny aspect of a country, a picture of one moment, at one place in time.

An interesting question I got was, "Are there any Muslims in America?" The very fact that they even ask that tells me we have much to learn about each other in the world. The last two weeks in Indonesia I wore a Muslim hat, mainly in honor of Ramadan, but also for my own curiosity to see how people would respond to a westerner wearing a Muslim hat. It was an interesting experience, and caught many people off guard that I would even have the desire to try and understand their religion. It broke down barriers rather quickly, and a nice bonus was many attractive young ladies told me that I looked pretty smart in the hat.

I don't have the desire to completely lose myself in a culture. For me, that would be like running away. But I do have a deep desire to understand differences, and to know the truth of a people—not just the fundamentalist factions who get all the press. All of the Islamic people I met were gracious and kind, and as one said to me, "It's like all religions in the world, whether Islam, Christian, Hindu, or any of them: you have some good people and some bad in each." Well said.

I was told that 1.3 million people canceled their vacations to Indonesia in 2001, and from what I experienced I think that figure must have been accurate. Often I would be the only person in a hotel. Places that are normally filled with back-packers were deserted. People would ask me as I moved around from place to place, "Aren't you afraid of sweeping?" I always asked if I should be. I was always told, "No, you don't have to be afraid here."

It turned out that the sweeping was always happening in the *next* town, but not where I was staying. And then when I would arrive in that town, it was always happening in the next, and so on. Bad press fueled so much of it, as the facts got lost in the mundane. But the kindness of people continued.

I paused briefly to consider teaching English in Indonesia. Indonesia has so much to offer. It has such diversity in people and places that at some point I would love to return to see the places I missed, to create new friendships and renew old ones. It will have to wait though, because inside of me, the pull to continue moving was ever-present.

I left Indonesia having found part of the innocence that lives in people; I also left with part of myself having found a place that felt like home.

Leaving Indo photographs [38], page 107 [39], page 107 [40], page 108 [41], page 109

Entry Twenty: A short stay in Malaysia

I spent only two days in Malaysia, then took an overnight bus to Thailand. It was expensive in Malaysia, and the people were not as friendly. Ramadan really filled the transportation systems, as everyone and their dog went home to be with their family for the end of the Holy Month.

It was another big city, and everything that that brings. Kuala Lumpur seemed to have nothing for me, yet I am sure that there are many amazing places in Malaysia.

So this can be a lesson to every fellow traveler: What happened inside me at the time I was in Malaysia, the feeling that I simply needed to move on, might have been entirely changed had I entered the country just a week before or a week after Ramadan. Please don't use my single experience as a reason not to explore Malaysia on your own, or to come to the wrong conclusion about this country. Go explore it and come to your own conclusion!

Entry Twenty-one: Holidays

On the road you get to choose your friends, and if you find someone you don't like, you just move on. No effort has to be made to get along or put up with annoyances out of obligation, or because you're stuck working with or even married to this person. It's a freedom that I cherished and exercised without any feelings of guilt. The journey moved too fast for that kind of drama. Having said that, there weren't many people that I didn't enjoy.

My time in southern Thailand was spent hanging out with a couple of characters named Warren and Kirsten. Warren is an ex-car dealer from England; Kirsten is an MD from Austria. They were great travel companions as we explored islands, caves and open-air markets. As a group we found the knack of being together, but also the ability to connect with those around us. The familiar pattern of saying goodbye repeated itself. You say goodbye, knowing the chances of seeing people again are rare, but you hope you do anyway.

Several moments stood out in southern Thailand, too many to mention them all. The five-island tour was good...tall island spires covered with vines and trees with small beaches dotted the seascape. The waters were warm, blue, full of fish and biting lice. Warren's back flips off the top of the boat were definitely worth noting.

In the town of Krabie, I visited a Buddhist temple twice. The second time I was alone, climbing the spire that held a temple at the top: 1,272 steps, straight up. I climbed above the sprawling green canopy that covered the flat land below. Alone, I sat there and watched the sun sink into the horizon. (I heard that if I listened closely, I might hear the plop of the sun as it dropped into the next day.) With the Buddhist bells ringing in the wind, the Indian Ocean and the golden landscape of spires, I sat there, next to a golden Buddha, and ended my day.

On Christmas Eve 2001, I found myself cruising along on a public ferry on one of the many rivers that cut through Bangkok, Thailand. There are officially 6 million people in Bangkok, and unofficially (as one cab driver told me) 15 million. Either way, it was a big city, and a stark contrast to the sleepy villages and small towns I had grown fond of.

From the time I arrived in Thailand I fell into the traveler's role, hanging out in touristy areas and chatting with other travelers. I found myself hungry to meet local people, but a heaviness seemed to have fallen over me; the effort to meet the locals seemed so large. It might have been a sign of holiday blues, or it might have been just a sign that I needed to take a little time to nourish my own body and spirit. But I was a bit unclear as to how to do that. Sitting in temples and churches offered some peace, but I sensed that I was missing the intimacy of physical touch. So I suspected a Thai massage was in order.

Back in the U.S. it is impossible to escape Christmas, with all of the advertising, shopping sales, music, and decorations. In Thailand, I had to look hard to find it. Thailand is 90% Buddhist, and Christmas is more of a reason to have a party than a holy holiday. In one sense, I enjoyed the absence of all the commercialism, the hurrying around and the frustration of not knowing what to buy. But I missed the excuse the holiday provides to be with family and friends, the laughter and good food.

Being away for Christmas in such a place as Bangkok put the celebration of Christmas back into the category of being a choice, not an obligation or commercial blur. I chose to attend a midnight mass to capture the spirit of Christmas unbound by borders, language or time.

"Christmas in Bangkok" sounds like a book or a song. For sure there's a poem in that somewhere. My midnight Christmas Eve service is a long tradition that started with my grandparents. Out of a sense of love and devotion to them, and to my relationship with Christ, I always attend. This service was held in a Catholic Church built in 1887, beautifully preserved, filled with local people. It was a perfect place for me. The service was in Thai; even the songs were in Thai. I hummed along to the familiar tunes. The last song of the service was in English: *Silent Night*. It was a tender moment, touching a familiar place in a foreign setting.

Then right before we were about to leave the service, they passed out a gift card and on the back of each card was a number. They proceeded to have a drawing and give away prizes. I found this a bit humorous, as the shy winners would walk up to claim their prizes with everyone clapping. I thought, "Well, this is fun." Then after an hour (at 2:30 AM,) they were *still* drawing numbers. I was thinking it was a plot to keep us there all night long...then it ended. (Yes, I won a prize, along with just about the entire congregation.)

To all who read this, may your holidays always be filled with the warmth and love that was and has always been intended for that time of year. May you have dreams of sweet things and songs that touch your hearts. May you have quiet moments of peace and the restful feelings that come when things are complete and done. And may you have love, for everything else is really just a blink in the eye of time.

Holidays photograph   [42], page 109

Entry Twenty-two: Chang Mai tourists

After Christmas, a friend came to join me and offer familiar company for the first time in some time.

With the arrival of my friend Ana, my trip took on a more typical tourist route (which it had already been traveling for a couple of weeks). Ana, from Costa Rica, flew in to do a little business combined with having a little fun. We headed north to Chiang Mai in an attempt to escape the pollution and large city of Bangkok.

We spent New Year's Eve on an overnight train to Chiang Mai. The clickety-clack of the train lulled us to sleep. (Far easier on my liver than past celebrations.) We ran into a little dilemma: Ana couldn't find her passport. The big push to figure out what to do about *that* began. Wow, if you ever travel, don't lose your passport! It's a totally time-consuming event. But we made the best of it, and "let go" of trying to force anything to happen. (That was good since a couple of days later it crawled back into the pocket of her small backpack.)

While in Chiang Mai, I rented a small motorbike, which we used one day to explore the area. Now, I'm no Easy Rider for sure, but I thought I could handle a small scooter. So, here we were riding up a highway on our way to a temple that we had heard about. I turned a corner, the road went straight up, second gear went nowhere, so I popped it into first. Well, that went somewhere without us. I popped a wheelie, and walked the bike up the hill for a brief moment before stopping.

I finally turned around to see this look of terror in Ana's eyes. Apparently she had fallen straight off the back of the bike onto the ground, and had popped up so fast that I never saw her. And me, well, I kind of laughed, not too loud, because what else are you going to do in that situation? Ana was a good sport about it. She found enough courage to hop back on the bike, and up we went.

The temple was packed with Buddhist worshipers beginning their new year with prayers and offerings to Buddha. Bells were ringing, flowers and incense abounded as crowds of people walked around the pagoda. Everyone wanted to attain some good luck from Buddha, so many offerings were made and presented.

Later we did a one-day trek, which included a ride on an elephant for a portion of the day. We had a frisky critter. For a moment I thought we were going to be in the elephant rodeo, because he had other ideas about where to go than where the guide had in mind. The day ended in a bamboo rafting trip. That part was real fun, balancing myself on this raft, traveling down small rapids, trying not to fall in and learning how to use a pole instead of a paddle. With no major accidents, we went home a little wet, and tired from a long day.

The other highlight of Chiang Mai was a cooking class. Yes, I know: those of you who know me well must be rolling on the floor laughing at the picture of me in a cooking class, given I can barely boil water. But, we all must start somewhere, and away I went. I love Thai food, so I wasn't going to pass up the chance to learn how to prepare it.

I actually learned quite a bit. Some of my classmates found it amusing that I would write in my notes things like: "Turn on stove," and "Turn off burner." But hey, it's not a natural thing for me. Maybe someday some of you will have the opportunity to taste my cooking. I'll let you be the judge of whether it's good or bad. But that day, it was good!

We returned to Bangkok and finished up the shopping for Ana. We sneaked in a day trip to a floating market and the bridge over the river Kwai (yes, the one from the movie). That part of the trip was solemn. To view the war museum and actually walk across the bridge brought the reality of war closer to home.

It is important to see such things as a reminder that war is not a story, but an event that can happen and should be avoided when at all possible. The other significance of this place has no deep meaning, but has a special memory for me. One weekend I went to visit my brother Dale at Wayne State College in Wayne, Nebraska. While there, one evening I was sitting in the TV room watching the movie *Bridge Over the River Kwai*. Dale was studying (which he always did), and I was watching the movie with another student nicknamed "Dirt." As we watched the movie, I glanced out to the hallway and asked, "Is it was always smoky like that?"

Dirt fell out of his chair, as he realized that there was a major fire going on somewhere in the dorm. As we all headed to the outside and cold air, I met some people who were to become my friends, forever. It was that weekend that I decided to attend college instead of joining the Air Force, which changed my life forever. So this place has added meaning to me. (No one was hurt in the fire that night, thankfully.)

After ten days, Ana returned to Costa Rica and I started the next leg of the journey. It was good to have the chance to spend a little time with my friend. But the familiar pull to get moving grew each day. Whispers in my ear said that there were things waiting for me, and growing impatient. I left for Laos, a country I kept hearing so many good things about.

Chang Mai tourists photograph   [43], page 110   [44], page 110

Entry Twenty-three: Laos

There was a calm in Laos. The quiet arose from the lack of cars and motorbikes. In turn, the quiet lent itself to a distinct peacefulness.

Don't get me wrong, though. The lack of infrastructure had its challenges and frustrations, but it was a welcome change from the buzz of Bangkok.

Arriving in Laos, I discovered the cheap ride up the Mekong River that I was planning on taking was no longer cheap. So, I opted for the bus. The bus there was a mini pickup truck with a blue plastic tarp over the back in case of rain. I got lucky and squeezed into the extended cab with two others. For eight hours I sat there like a sardine in a can with my knees in my face. Occasionally I would straighten my legs, which brought much laughter from my Laos riding mates, as my back would parallel the cab roof. Every two or three hours we stopped for a bathroom break or to eat, either of which gave me a chance to escape my little cage.

The scenery was endless forest and jungle. The views were amazing and satisfied my desire to see forest that was untouched by clear-cutting and deforesting. The road ran past villages that had no electricity. Children smiled and yelled "goodbye" instead of hello. At one point we dropped off a passenger at one of the villages, which allowed for a rest break. There, I took a brief walk to explore the area. You could tell that most trucks didn't stop there from the looks of curiosity and shy, smiling children poking their heads around corners for a peek. I found myself wishing I could stay and play, but soon the horn was honking and I was off again.

After spending a couple of days in Muang Sing, in way northern Laos, I left a little disappointed. The villages I trekked through had seen many tourists, and I was left with the feeling they were only interested in selling me something or charging me to take their photo. Even with that, it was interesting. The hill tribal villagers wore authentic clothing, multiple colors, and they had a lot of character in their faces. It was a mixed bag, but I was glad I went. Many times I was offered opium by little old ladies with no teeth and big grins. They would approach me making a sound like "Kaw ja, Kaw ja." I have nothing to report here; it's not my thing to smoke, but now I can say I've seen it.

My first night in Mue Sing was not very restful. Rats ran through the walls, and my neighbor stayed busy with his temporary company. I draped my mosquito net for some mental peace of mind, knowing full well that a rat could chew through it in an instant. Throughout the night I would wake up to a rustling noise. Soon I discovered that the rats were playing on my nightstand next to my bed, chewing on my things. The little buggers even chewed up the cord that held my sunglasses around my neck! The electricity went out at 10:30 PM, so the best option was to light a candle, hoping to keep them at bay. The rats seemed happy about that, because it allowed them to see better after I fell asleep. I found a new guesthouse for the next night.

After catching a bus back to the Mekong River, I soon found myself with a small group bouncing down the river in a speedboat. The Mekong is a serious river, and I was happy to be wearing a lifejacket as we scooted over rapids and giant whirlpools, dodging rocks and rock outcrops at 80 kilometers an hour. Eventually we made it to Huay Xai, the point where I began my northern Laos journey. Here we were given the surprise and news of no boat traffic being allowed on the river because the Laotian president was meeting with Vietnam's president.

With no other option but to wait, I surrendered to the fact that I would be there for two more days. Wandering around town, I became friends with some local Buddhist monks. With time on my hands, I offered to be a guest English teacher for the novices. This was greeted with much delight, to have a native English speaker teaching class. Finally, a chance to use my TESOL (Teacher of English to Speakers of Other Languages). (Bernice, you would have been proud.) For two hours we practiced (and hopefully, they acquired some) English. They were the most polite students imaginable as they sat there smiling in their orange robes; shy, but eager to learn.

I loved it as much as they did. It was my chance to give to, and connect with, the everyday people of Laos for a brief moment.

Departing Huay Xai, I continued down the Mekong River. I escaped being put on the tourist boat, where they herded tourist like cattle, and I slipped onto a local water taxi. The taxi was a boat with windows (unlike the other, which had none). A young Australian man named Oliver and his friend, a young German woman named Charlotte, followed my lead. So it was us three with the locals.

For two days we moved slowly down the Mekong River, stopping occasionally to pick up or drop off people. It was some of the most relaxing travel I've ever had. I read my book, or took a nap, or just watched the countryside float by. At one point we came across a number of elephants being used to load a ship along the bank. We were treated to scenes of everyday life along the Mekong: naked children playing along the shore, water buffalo grazing by its side, woman washing clothes, people bathing. It was a good ride.

In Luang Prabang I found a warm shower and good food. I also met up with a local man whom I had met earlier in Muang Sing, a tour guide named Mr. Udong. I located Mr. Udong's home and found him celebrating the official holiday for the military with several friends, the chief of the police and a few other chiefs that I can't remember. They sat in a circle knocking back shots of Lao Lao, a rice wine. Well, by noon I was done.

Realizing I had to escape, I excused myself under the guise of going sightseeing. Walking down the street I wandered into a Buddhist temple and started chatting with the monks, who were always eager to practice their English. Expressing how tired I felt, they opened up the temple door and told me to sack out for a while on the floor. After 1 1/2 hours, I awoke refreshed and finished my exploration of Laung Prabang. It was the end of what felt to be a very long day.

Before I left Mr. Udong's home that day, he insisted that I return the second night for a traditional Laotian dinner. So I returned to Mr Udung's home one more time, with a little trepidation I must add, for the dinner date. It was a festive and ceremonial occasion. He had invited all of his family members to dinner along with a few neighbors, including the police chief and his wife.

We all sat in the center of the floor around a round bamboo table. In the center of the table was a very ornate table setting that included a candle, flowers and sticks with several pieces of twine tied around them. Surrounding the base of the setting were various types of food. We all leaned forward and a blessing was given, along with well wishes for the evening and for having friends. Then they took turns placing some of the food on my lap, giving more blessings. After that, they took the strings off the stick and each took turns tying one on each of my wrists.

Looking at me in my eyes, smiling, they tied a string and said a blessing which generally included, "Safe journey to you," "May you find much happiness," "May you find much wealth," "May your family be blessed." Mr. Udung translated some of it as it was happening; otherwise it was all in Laotian, but my heart understood it all.

I ended up with ten string twines on each wrist. It was so heartwarming to receive so much love from those whom I hardly knew. It taught me how to receive gracefully. They explained to me that it was a tradition to send friends and family off on a journey with this type of ceremony. Then we ate and took more shots of Lao Lao to celebrate the event. It was a wonderful night.

On my way to Vientiane, I spent a night in Vang Vieng, a kind of halfway point. The morning I left, I awoke early to walk through the markets and take some photos. As I strolled along I came across a couple of tables under a tin roof that appeared to be the local coffee shop, so I slid in for a cup.

The street was full of women selling food items and produce. The coffee shop was full of half-shaven, smiling (teeth optional) old men wearing funny hats and glasses, chatting about who knows what—but I can imagine. The scene was not so different from the one I experienced at a local coffee shop in Spencer, Nebraska, back home when I visited my friend Jim. There were lively discussions, laughter, and debating.

The only word they spoke that I understood was "Ovaltine," which occurred after I ordered a cup. It was accompanied with some laughter. You see, Ovaltine is hot chocolate. I'm sure had I ordered the same in Spencer, it probably would have received the same response.

I took a photo of my table mates before I left. That way, I can send it to Spencer someday to be put up in the local coffee shop there just to show how similar the world really is. We tried to chat but they spoke no English, so I said "thank you" and "goodbye" (some of the only Laotian words I know) and caught my bus south.

Laos is a wonderful country to visit. Mostly it's the people that make it special; they are kind and peaceful. "Laid back" would be a good description. The countryside is mostly untouched, what little I really saw. It's a backpacker's travel dream: cheap and beautiful.

I took a short flight to Hanoi, Vietnam. It was one of the rare times I chose to fly; the trip across land was just too much. Plus, it would have involved too much backtracking—something I avoid as much as possible.

The plane ride took me back to the west, although briefly. Familiar food came to me on plastic trays. I reclined my seat for a moment and reflected on how this scene contrasted with what I'd just experienced in Laos. My two weeks there had been rough, rugged and exciting. The flight to Hanoi felt good. It was wonderful to be waited on and to have a stress-free exchange of service. I was wise enough to realize, however, that the flight was quite temporary.

I avoided getting attached to that lifestyle in that hour of comfort. Besides, for me it becomes boring too quickly. I was ready to go back to living on ten dollars a day by the time we touched down in Hanoi.

Laos photograph [45], page 110

Entry Twenty-four: Vietnam

Vietnam began for me with the loss of a full hour's worth of Web site typing somewhere in cyberspace. AUGHH!, as Lucy would say.

Hanoi, Vietnam, was an interesting blend of ancient and modern, all going a hundred miles an hour. The relief of fewer cars on the street was more than made up for by a flood of motorbikes going everywhere. The sea of motorbikes was interwoven with women carrying yokes on their shoulders, balanced by two baskets hanging on each end, which were filled with everything imaginable. The amount of weight they carried was enormous, and once they started walking they had a skip in their walk that seemed to carry them right along.

Hanoi also had a unique buzz of commerce. There weren't the neon signs of McDonalds or Kentucky Fried Chicken, but there was no lack of opportunity to eat or buy whatever I wanted. I liked Hanoi, partly because it was so different, yet offered so much. The people were friendly; sometimes a bit persistent in trying to sell me something, but they had a lot of character, which created an interesting experience. The city was charming in spite of the communist-inspired gray concrete buildings that were, frankly, drab.

One of my first stops was to go visit the "Hanoi Hilton"—not the real Hilton, but the prison De Hoc Lo. This was where the North Vietnamese kept pilots shot down during the Vietnam War. (By the way, the Vietnamese call that conflict "The American War.") This was the place where Senator John McCain was kept after being shot down. Seeing this place gave me a whole new appreciation for Senator McCain, and the amount of determination he had to survive.

The prison conditions and prisoner treatment were horrible. Beds slanted towards the head so the body's blood went to the prisoners' heads when they lay down. Prisoners wore leg shackles. Unspeakable things were done to break the spirits of the prisoners. It left me wishing McCain was our President, just out of sheer toughness. Bush is no McCain. (But that's another story, and if anyone is ever interested in what the world thinks of Bush, email me and I'll be happy to share.)

The mausoleum of Ho Chi Minh was an experience all to itself. People filed by his body in silence. It had a spooky feeling to it, but I wouldn't have missed it. There he was, on display, almost godlike for the people of Vietnam: Uncle Ho.

I've discovered that part of me searches for that which is familiar even in unfamiliar places. It happens with everyone I meet, as I approach people with the understanding that we share the same qualities of what it means to be a part of the human race. This keeps things simple, and has a magical quality of putting people at ease.

Sometimes it expressed itself as I searched out a Catholic cathedral in the middle of Hanoi on a Saturday night where not a word of English was spoken except, "Amen." I have found it unnecessary to understand the words of the mind if the heart is open to receive. And thus the cycle continues.

Heading north out of Hanoi, I went in search of terraced rice fields, quiet valleys and silent nights. I found it in the mountains of Sapa in a small, charming village on the Chinese border, perched high in the mountains, filled with local hill tribes selling their goods. But I hungered for something else, something less exposed to so many tourists. I hired a guide and requested to be taken to the places less visited.

After a long bumpy ride on the back of a small motorbike and a long walk, I found myself in a more remote village that would serve as our base camp. A hiking companion named Josh and I immediately embarked on a trek, after dumping some items at our guesthouse. Soon I was surrounded by terraced rice fields, walking along a path next to a river that had only farmers and occasional children. After trekking for several hours, our guide walked up to a farmhouse, chatted with the farmers for a few moments and then waved us in.

Although our guide had never met them before, it didn't matter. They still lived in a time where travelers weren't really strangers, and soon we found ourselves sitting next to the fire preparing lunch. The house was more like a barn with chickens and other animals walking freely around the dirt floors, making their way around the farm tools scattered about.

Our hosts were part of the Hmong hill tribes, and before too long, Hmong wine was being poured out. Uh-oh, here we go. It wasn't long before my guide and hiking companion were rip-roaring drunk. I took one shot of the homemade wine to be polite, but that was it. It tasted like rubbing alcohol with corn dust mixed in for flavor.

From there we headed home. As I watched my two companions stumble home down the muddy trail I thought, "They're going to be hurting in the morning."

The next day we got up early, a big surprise to me, and hopped onto the back of some motorbikes once again. This time we reached a village where no one tried to sell me a thing, or ask me for a pencil. Here, people looked at us with curiosity and shyness.

Once again our guide procured a kitchen and went about making lunch, and while he did that I went exploring. I found a school, and soon found myself teaching English. After an hour of that, I had the entire school out in the schoolyard in a huge circle and taught them the Hokey Pokey. The many villagers looking on found great amusement in watching this westerner do this funny song and dance, and the students followed my lead, filled with laughter all the way.

Soon it was time to leave. As I left, the students were shouting "Ciao, Dean! Ciao, Dean!" as I waved goodbye. I'd found an avenue that allowed me to share, laugh and connect with young people.

I'd anticipated that the train ride back to Hanoi would be on "soft seats" as I requested when I purchased my ticket. But I arrived at the train car to discover that there were no "softs" anywhere on the train, only hard wooden benches. And so, the next 12 hours began. My train car was the second to the last, followed by the luggage car. Now *that* was the car where all the action was happening. It was a zoo on wheels.

Crates of chickens and pigs on their way to some market, motorbikes, huge bags of rice and boxes of who-knows-what were stacked to the ceiling. It truly was a *National Geographic* moment. On top of that were all the vendors. They jammed back into the car, for reasons I still haven't figured out.

The old man in charge of our car yelled and pushed them back through the doorway. In turn, they would yell back and laugh at him, sticking their feet in the door as he tried to shut it. All kinds of hands and arms flew around; it was great to watch. Then the old man would walk back through our car and smile at all of us, shaking our hands like nothing was happening. It helped pass the time on a long, hard-seated journey.

Coming to Vietnam I wasn't sure what to expect. My concepts and ideas of the country had been shaped so much by the movies and news media over time. Ignorance is no excuse, but at least it can be addressed with an open mind to understand. Part of me expected to see limbless, disfigured bodies— casualties of the ugly war in large numbers. And while I did find those people, I had to look very hard for them. I don't remember studying much about the war, for I was of the age in-between: too young to fight, and too young for it to be in my history books.

In addition, I was too distracted by the everyday happenings of life to care much. Not something to be very proud of, but that's my own internal question of, why at that point, didn't I really take notice of what was happening. As I planned my trip, I knew I had to come to Vietnam, if for nothing else than to try and come to grips with an event that just doesn't want to heal itself in my home country. What is it about the Vietnam War that seems to keep a clear understanding of what happened so elusive?

Being there gave me a fraction of deeper understanding. It was educational to hear the other side's viewpoint, even though I had to sift through the propaganda. (That being said, the U.S. government is very good at producing its own propaganda. So it's fair play.)

I spent a day touring the old DMZ (demilitarized zone). We toured an old military base called Khe Sanh Combat Base. Our guide, who was very well read on what both sides have written about the war, turned us loose to wander around the area and museum. On the walls of the museum were many photographs touting the Liberation Army's victories. They pulled no punches about their feelings toward what they called the Imperialist American Army. Fair enough; it was their museum. Besides, I can see through propaganda when it's in front of me—no matter what country it's from.

While we were there, another tour bus full of Americans pulled up. Some of the tourists from that bus strolled in, being a bit too loud and obnoxious. Unfortunately, I found that to be a trend in American groups visiting other countries.

One of the women in the group suddenly roared with laughter. "They make it sound like it was miserable for us here." The level of ignorance and arrogance was just too much for me and I snapped at her, "Of course it was miserable here, and it's really not a funny situation."

She tried to ignore me, as some of her group members tried to justify her stupidity by explaining that a couple of the members on their tour actually had spent time in the war. The only other words I could get out were, "You're very sad." Someone else piped in and said, "I agree."

When people from the other group picked up the museum guns that were a part of a display and started playing with them, I had to leave. As I did, someone in my group spoke to me, while rolling his eyes, saying; "Now you can see why much of the world has, at times, a hard time with Americans."

It hit a core button in me. I was ashamed of the museum tourists and their lack of humility, a quality all of us as Americans could stand a dose of. My own conclusion is that we as a country are very generous, but when driven by the big ego of wanting attention for it, that generosity serves to inflate that big ego instead of nurturing a genuine place of empathy and humility.

I also believe we will someday learn to nurture empathy as a nation. Maybe it won't happen in my lifetime, but it will happen. I have known many people who don't fit that perceived American trend and I have more faith in them than those of the trend.

The other conclusion is the obvious: many people suffered from and during the war. Many Vietnamese told me, "Live and let live, you and I can be friends." I believe that to be a sincere offer, one that can help everyone move forward, learn from a dark time, and have us look towards a world that can live in peace. To have local people, complete strangers, tell me how sorry they were about the September 11th event after they found out I was from the United States, tells me we have a chance at that peace. Pain can either divide us or unite us as humanity. The choice will always be there.

In Hoi An, I was reunited with Warren, my English friend I met in southern Thailand. Seeing Warren was like finding a long lost friend. As a team we were magic, playing with the local people and having fun.

In Hoi An, we also celebrated Tet, the Chinese New Year. This is the biggest celebration of the year for Vietnam. It's a combination of Christmas, New Year's, Easter and Happy Birthday all thrown into three days. People unite with their families, visit friends and put on their best clothes.

I was invited to a local family's home as their first guest of the year, a symbolic moment. They want people who are lucky to be the first guest in the hope that the guest's luck will be rubbed off onto the household. So after performing the customary ritual of greetings, we sat down for tea and breakfast. Afterwards our host, Thun, said it was time to go see his grandparents, and away we went.

Hopping on my motorbike, winding down small pathways, we rode to his grandparents' house. It was a bit of a shock to me to find his grandparents consisted of two altars on the wall, dedicated to them. The way he had spoken about them, I had thought they were still alive.

The Vietnamese believe that during Tet all of their past ancestors return, as well as those still living, to their homes. So this was a very natural expression of his beliefs and a wonderful experience for me. Throughout the day we visited family and friends, went to Buddhist temples to pay tribute to the past and pray for good luck in the future. It was a good day.

My last day in Hoi An, Warren, my two German friends Sophie and Simone, and I rented motorbikes for a trip to Marble Mountain. Marble Mountain is a Buddhist shrine with altars inside a hollowed-out mountain. The place was extra busy with local people for Tet, lighting incense, praying, and making offerings.

The cave inside was quite large, and at the top there were openings that allowed sunlight to pour in and illuminate the smoke-filled air like beams from heaven. The place had a sacred presence to it, with all the smells and special light.

While trying to capture the scene on film, way at the top of the cave, I noticed something floating down very slowly. At first I thought it was some ash that had floated up from one of the burnt offerings, because it just seemed to float as it basked in the rays of the sun. For several minutes I just sat there watching it, for it had completely captured me as the background scene melted away. Eventually, and so slowly, it began to float closer to the ground. As it did, I walked slowly across the cave towards the floating object, arriving at the same spot and at the same time. I held out my hand and this beautiful seed, shaped like a large dandelion seed, landed gently in the palm of my hand. Like a letter sent from heaven, I gratefully received the token, and said "Thank you." A young local girl stood there watching me. Her wide-open eyes were filled with amazement. I would have loved to know what she was thinking.

After exploring Marble Mountain we left for China Beach, a once-famous resting place for American soldiers. Here I skillfully got my motorbike waterlogged. Warren and I provided the locals with a great deal of entertainment as we kept trying to push start the bike, backfiring down the road. Eventually with some cleaning and drying out it started again, and we went home.

Walking or riding in the streets of Vietnam is another experience all to itself. The only rule: the biggest guy has the right of way. Like currents in a stream, motorbikes and bicycles are flowing every which way. Just like when the current changes if you drop a stone in a stream, it's the same for riding in the streets of Vietnam. Still, the system seems to work—mostly because everything is moving so slow.

The night before I left Hoi An, I got very sick. Poor Warren had to listen to me chat on deliriously for hours until he finally fell asleep. I had a major fever, shaking with chills, sheets wet from sweating and blankets piled on because I felt so cold. I'll never forget the strange sense I felt lying in bed at 4 AM, my mind a bit twisted from the fever and hearing the sound of a distant bell from a Buddhist temple. It was as if I had been there before and I was watching a movie of the past, yet I was in a strange place far from home. At 6 AM, I slowly pulled myself onto the bus, wondering what the next 12 hours would bring. Luckily, the bus was half full, which gave me a row of seats to myself. I slept a good deal of the way, much to the disgust of the others on the bus who found it impossible to sleep.

I found my way to Na Thrang, where Sophie and Simone could help take care of me. They watched over me the next few days as I mended slowly. On a better day I rented a motorbike because I'd found Neta, my long lost friend and travel mate from Indonesia again. Neta and I went in search of ordinary Vietnam.

We soon found ourselves lost in a fishing village and being invited into the home of a sweet Vietnamese girl. Insisting we stay for lunch, we got to learn about her and her father. It was like other moments once you get away from the tourist path. You can meet so many friendly and sincere people.

After several hours it was time to leave, and after the customary photo, we said goodbye. Once again I was touched by the friendliness and kindness of those in a country where you'd think American-hating could be a national pastime.

My reunion with Neta was brief and sweet, like finding a favorite T-shirt you thought was forever lost, and then putting it back in the drawer until the next time.

And off to Saigon went Simone, Sophie and I. (Me and my nursemaids.) Saigon, officially known now as Ho Chi Min City, is another full-on city, bustling and hustling all hours of the day. Saigon also revealed to me some of its turbulent past. Most notable was the Reunification Palace, which housed the old offices of the South Vietnamese government. Eerily preserved as it was on the day it fell to the North Vietnamese in 1975, it was like walking back in time. You could still sense the despair they must have felt. The feeling of defeat still lingered in the air. The war museum there was also quite striking, full of propaganda and photos of the Vietnam War.

It is my heart's wish that we never have to endure another day of tragedy such as this war. Such horrific things happened during this event. Let us learn from it and remain committed to creating peace.

When I left Saigon I had to say goodbye to my two lovely German angels, to whom I will remain indebted for watching over my sick body. We laughed a lot. I still miss that.

A forgotten wake-up call left me scrambling to catch my bus my final morning there. Hopping onto the bus as it was pulling away, I headed for the Mekong Delta and a rendezvous with a boat to take me up the river to Cambodia.

Vietnam is a country full of grace and intense character. The women are so beautiful, I found it easy to understand why so many American soldiers fell in love and got married. The food was plentiful and excellent. The people shared their hearts and thus touched mine. The future of Vietnam looks more promising than its past. Hopefully, it will change without sterilizing the wonderful culture.

And the people? As they told me many times, "Me and you can be friends."

Vietnam photographs

Entry Twenty-five: Life lessons in Cambodia

My trip up the Mekong was like a quiet journey through a forgotten time. The bank was lined with houses and fields, as it had been for many years. Everything looked timeless yet temporary, I imagine, thanks to the annual high water that often carries away the houses.

The people of the Mekong rebuild year after year, in the same place and the same way. Women doing laundry, people bathing, children playing, others squatting to go to the bathroom—all life here revolves around the Mekong River. Touching millions of lives, the Mekong truly is a grand river in the scheme of things.

The boat took us to the border of Cambodia, where we disembarked and passed through customs and immigration. Having been on the boat for several hours watching life from a distance, it was difficult to note any changes between Cambodia and Vietnam. But when we arrived at the border town, I definitely felt a difference. There was a different sense in the air, not so recognizable to me: a heaviness behind the smiles and kindness of the people.

Thus my time in Cambodia began. I found myself ignorant of its past and uncertain of what lay ahead. Cambodia has left a mark on me, one that will take some time to digest. I will try to share why, and what I continue to try and come to grips with.

My main priority in Cambodia was to walk through and experience the wonders of Angkor Wat, the city of the ancient Khmer people who created an astounding civilization. I had been hearing about Angkor for some time on my journey from other travelers who had already been there. It didn't take long for me to realize I had to go there myself.

Whatever else Cambodia had to offer was a complete mystery to me. This forced me, once again, to address how little I know about the world. Sometimes I wondered if this trip would have been better for someone with more knowledge of the past, someone that might have a deeper appreciation of the details of such a place. But there I was, and learn I did, from observing and engaging in the world around me. I trusted it was no accident that I was there. It was my responsibility to discover why, and that was enough for the moment.

When I arrived in Phnom Pehn I rented a motorcycle. Okay, make that a dirt bike, because the roads are horrible in Cambodia. Then I watched the movie *The Killing Fields*. This was the beginning of my discovering Cambodia's national nightmare.

Early the next morning, I set off alone to learn for myself just what happened here. I started at the S 21 prison, now a genocide museum that displays the horrific efforts of Pol Pot to rid the country of "capitalist-contaminated" people. Of the 20,000 prisoners, which included women and children and a few westerners, only five survived. What once was a school was converted into a nightmare that my words will never be able to communicate.

On the walls hung the photographs of those who lived behind the barbed wire and bars until their time came to go to the killing fields. I will spare the details; there are plenty of books available that can give that information. But in S 21, I began to understand the heaviness I felt: it was the aftershock that lingers in a nation that eliminated 20% of its population for reasons that will never be reconcilable. The brightest and most promising were exterminated out of a twisted and dark experiment to reverse time and create the model communist state.

After the museum, I rode out to a genocidal museum created at one of the killing fields. The centerpiece of the museum was a large tower with glass walls. Inside the walls were several shelves crowded with 8,000 human skulls retrieved from nearby mass graves. As I silently strolled through the area, traces of human bones could be seen scattered across the ground. This was not a place for the squeamish, but everyone should be exposed to the truth in some way. It is our best defense that this will never happen again.

Afterwards I sat at the edge of the killing fields on the steps of the large tower, in a bit of shock. Where had I been from 1975 to 1979, when this was all happening? Why didn't I take notice of such a horrible thing and be moved to do something about it? How can we as a human race just stand by and let something like this happen?

The day left me troubled with hard questions. Words of Buddha floated through my mind, "This is a place of suffering." I thought, "How true, but this is needless suffering in the worst and largest way imaginable."

It is a lesson we cannot afford to miss. It is truth we cannot let slip into denial, and thus be forgotten.

On a brighter note, I met an American family traveling together—the Nolans. Mike a high school counselor, Ann a high school teacher. Their three children Jay (14), Lucy (13), and Madeline (11) were an inspiration to me. Given that 80% of Americans do not possess a passport, I found this family to be remarkable. They were in the middle of a 14-month trip abroad. I was so proud of them, and thus adopted them. We traveled together for a short period of time, and I look forward to seeing them again someday back in Port Angeles, Washington. It inspired me in that, yes, you can travel *and* have an adventurous life *and* be married with children.

We finally came to Angkor Wat. With a few signs of the sickness I'd picked up in Vietnam still lingering in me, I walked through the ancient and almost forgotten temples of this once great civilization. It reminded me of scenes from an Indiana Jones movie. These incredible temples spanned across acres of ground surrounded by huge moats that were once filled with crocodiles. Like a storybook transformed to reality, life-size carvings and buildings that took years to create present themselves to those who come to Angkor Wat.

Although Angkor Wat is "touristy," because of its immense size, it's very easy to find a quiet corner and imagine what life must have been like so long ago. And even though time has passed, it still carries an air of majesty. I can see why it has inspired so many. Some temples are being restored, while others remain just as they were found, with trees growing over the ancient walls as the jungle reclaims what was once its own.

Even though I fell asleep waiting for my guide at one point (from just being exhausted and sick), Angkor did not disappoint. I was happy I came, and when the time came, I was happy to go. I felt like I was full; filled with what Southeast Asia wanted to give me, and fulfilled in what I had given in return. The mountains of Nepal were calling and I knew it was time to go.

Life lessons in Cambodia photographs   [54], page 115   [55], page 116   [56], page 116

Entry Twenty-six: Kathmandu

Well, there I was in Nepal—Kathmandu, to be precise.

Just the name Kathmandu strikes up images of faraway exotic things. Maybe the fact that Nepal is home to eight of the ten highest mountains in the world is part of its appeal. In any case, Nepal has been able to capture the hearts of adventurous types for a long time.

But first I must back up for a moment. Just *getting* to Nepal was a small adventure. From Bangkok I flew Bangladesh Airlines, the cheapest ticket available. It included an overnight stay in Bangladesh. A bit exhausted from the last few weeks, I fell asleep straight away, even before the plane left the runway. So, when we landed, I rubbed my eyes, grabbed my day pack, and followed the crowd leaving the plane.

As I left someone spoke something to me in broken English. I just nodded, because I had no idea what city we were supposed to land in; I just knew it should be somewhere in Bangladesh. So, I headed off with the crowd, got in line for immigration and started filling out the entry card. I thought to myself, "How strange. The card says Myanmar. They must be using some leftover cards."

A few minutes went by as I moved closer to the entry post. Suddenly several Bangladesh Airlines crew members came dashing in, looking for me. I had gotten off at the wrong country. We were in Myanmar, not Bangladesh! (Whoops.)

The Burmese soldiers were quite amused by it all as, eager to practice their English, they sat there chatting with me. The Bangladesh Airline folks gave me dirty looks as I returned to the plane, probably because it created a nasty paperwork error for them. I just smiled, slipped into my seat and fell back asleep, trusting the next time they'd wake me up when it was time to leave.

When I bought the ticket, no one mentioned the several stops before our final destination in Bangladesh. Or the fact that they would confiscate my passport and keep it at some airport desk during my overnight stay, but nonetheless, I made it to Nepal.

Flying in that morning gave me goose bumps. It was as if I was flying through the heavens and the gods themselves had come out to welcome me into their residence. Majestic clouds woven through monumental mountains welcomed me into the next step of my journey. This awoke the sleeping dream of adventure in me to explore the world's highest mountains.

I have never lived with the delusion of wanting to climb Mt. Everest. Coupled with the fact that it would cost $20,000-$50,000 which is totally crazy, many people die up there. (The latter still seems to be a strong enough deterrent for me.) My dream was to go to the base camp. That journey would be enough to quench my mountain hunger, at least for now.

I did two treks in Nepal. The first trek was called the Annapurna Circuit. This route covers a large loop around the Annapurna Mountains. Stephen Camron, a friend from Paris, joined me for this trek. I first met Stephen in San Diego several years ago. He was a great hiking partner, in better shape than I, and walked much faster than I could. In addition, he's a doctor, so he could pronounce me dead if necessary.

Leaving Kathmandu early one morning, we set off with no guide, no porter, just a map that had hilarious sidebars: "stone steps," "area of bandits," "hike in group," and the like.

Taking the bus as far as possible, riding on the roof at times and ducking under tree branches, we eventually got on the trail at 3 PM. Finally. The trek is 350 kilometers long. Some people do it in as little as 14 days. (Why, I have no idea.) Others take up to 28 days. While we were on the trek, a race around the circuit was going on. Those trekkers did it in nine days. They were mostly French, which explained a lot.

As I walked along the trek, I couldn't stop smiling. I was almost giddy over the fact that I was trekking through the Himals. It was such a distant dream of mine to see the Himalayans, I had to keep pinching myself and saying out loud, "I'm in the Himalayan Mountains, I'm in the Himalayan Mountains." Each day we would hike four to six hours, making our way higher and higher, the scenery ever-changing. Moving from tropics to Alpine, from Alpine to just plain cold.

One of the many things that struck me was the abundance of butterflies; their shapes, sizes and colors were endless. At times it was like walking through a moving garden of these little messengers of encouragement.

As we moved higher, the temperatures moved in the opposite direction. Warm sunny days and cold clear nights. A community of people began to form on the trek. Throughout the day we would leap frog each other and generally stop for lunch or stay in the same locations. (Some we got to know well enough that when we saw them in a lodge, we would stay somewhere else.)

Occasionally in the evenings, I would walk through the villages to chat with local people. One evening I started playing hide and seek with the children, and before long the whole village was playing as we dashed through people's homes and sheds. It filled the night with smiles and laughter.

On the way to Thorung La Pass, we started trekking with Ami and Ren, a young couple from Wisconsin. It turned out that they loved cribbage, so at night and throughout the day we would play—sometimes for hours. Generally you wake up at 6 AM, you're on the trail by 7 and arrive at your target destination by early afternoon to beat the afternoon clouds and potential rain or snow. This left large gaps of time to fill with no TV—just a book or cards or chatting. I've never had such an easy time waking up at 6:30, and those who know me well understand that this is a big deal, but then again, I've never regularly gone to bed at 7 PM either. Meals usually consisted of dalbhat, a rice and beans combo, with a few veggies on the side. It was what the locals ate, so it was generally safe to eat and fresh.

One night Stephen and I were lying on our beds when we heard some machine gun fire in the village where we were staying. Nepal was in the midst of some internal political problems. We were aware of it, but weren't concerned until then. The sound startled us, and we proceeded to have a conversation about an escape plan if needed. Stephen voted for the bushes in the hills; I voted for the closest trail that led out of town ASAP. Thankfully, we never had to implement either plan. We encountered a number of army personnel on the trek, but never felt unsafe, just a little uneasy.

On the trail I came to a Y intersection. Stephen was ahead of me, and we had discussed taking a certain path. All paths led to the next campsite, so that part was handled. At that moment I was trekking with a group of slower walkers, and one of them had a guide who suggested the low route. Supposedly it was shorter. The second he said that, I was for it. Only thing was, Stephen was ahead of me—and how far ahead I didn't know.

"Oh well," I told myself, "it will all work out." So away we went, skirting along a ridge that had a very steep drop to the bottom far below. We came to a section of the trail that was in poor condition, probably one of the reasons this trail was supposed to be closed. I jumped across loose rocks, moving as fast I could to the next secure location. While I waited in this spot for a moment I noticed a herd of mountain sheep high above our group, moving parallel to us. As they moved, they began kicking up large rocks that came tumbling down the mountainside like rockets. Those often knocked larger rocks loose, making for a very dangerous situation.

I hunkered down behind a large boulder, while flying rocks whizzed by me on all sides. "Jeesh," I thought, "what a bad idea this is!" As I sat there, one of my climbing companions came up the trail and stopped just across from me on the edge of the tricky area. I looked up and spied a large rock coming down the mountain, kicking up dust and making thud noises. I screamed at her to duck and take cover. Just as she did a large boulder zipped right over the top of her head. "Oh man, we've got to get out of here!" I said.

And after the sheep moved on to a new spot, we all watched above for one another until we reached a safe location. Eventually we arrived at the last camping area before climbing over the pass. One problem was immediate: Stephen had not yet arrived. I sat outside waiting for him, hoping he was all right, and feeling very guilty for taking a different path without telling him. On the other side of the valley I finally spotted what looked like him coming this way.

When he finally got to the camping area, he was upset and understandably so. He had waited for me, thinking I was in some kind of trouble. He even looked for me before finally moving on. After I explained about what had happened, and how my warning had kept one of our climbing companions from buying the proverbial farm, he forgave me. He even shared in our relief that we were both all right.

At one point on the trek, we crossed over a mountain pass called Thorung La Pass. Sitting at a mere 17,765 feet, the Thorung La would make this day the greatest challenge of the trek. Altitude becomes a real concern at that height, and precautions are needed to avoid having problems and potential dangers. This pass is 3,000 feet higher than Mt. Rainier in the state of Washington, which dominates the horizon of the Northwest.

The night before we ascended the pass, I got sick with a stomach bug. This meant I would begin the trek dehydrated, because it was coming out the back door faster then I could refill it through the front. Combined with air that was very short on oxygen, each step became an effort. It was as if molasses had replaced my blood. Slowly, but surely, I worked my way to the pass.

Waking up at 5 AM and leaving at 6 AM, we began the ten-hour day as morning's first light began to hit the tips of the highest mountains. Climbing through snow and over ice made the mountain seem inhospitable. Then, for a brief moment, you were allowed to see into the realm of another world where the gods call home—a place both breathtakingly beautiful and harshly unforgiving. As far as you could see, it was mountains, snow, ice and rock. The vegetation had long ago stopped on the trail, leaving only the hardiest life forms to fight it out with the elements. No more butterflies.

My heart was pounding. I wish I could say it was totally from excitement, but in truth it was mostly from the sheer effort I had to put forth to get to the top. And to the top we did make it (with me bringing up the rear, of course). Late morning came, and so did the obligatory photos of reaching the top. From there it was almost all downhill—six hours worth of knee-pounding downhill trekking, in fact.

My comrades, moving much quicker than I, jetted ahead of me at their own pace. At one point I was moving extra slow, and I came upon two Eastern Bloc European women relieving themselves. They were huge—weightlifters in my mind—so huge that my effort to ignore them failed. They greeted my arrival. Soon they were walking up from behind me. Noticing my slow pace, they asked if I was all right. Then one of them said, "Yuv vollow us, ve'll take care of vu".

"Yikes!" I thought. "They're going to turn me into an Eastern Bloc sandwich! No thanks!" Suddenly I felt better and sped off down the trail. Eventually I came crawling into our next guesthouse, exhausted to the core, but still alive.

The trek was constantly changing. On this side of the pass, everything changed again: villages, climate, vegetation. It was much drier. It was more Tibetan. For two days we walked in a riverbed. Dust blew in our faces; there was no shower available, just dirt. After a while you get used to it, but when that shower did come, wow! I suspect everyone was happy about that.

Throughout the days, Stephen and I discussed the merits of trekking. There was the obvious value of physical exercise outside in such a beautiful place. There was the grace of things being boiled down to the basics in a world that is striving to be so complex. It is in these moments that I have gained clarity on what's really important, what really counts. And it is in these moments the burden becomes lighter and more precious. Staying true to your own heart becomes easier, with fewer distractions to cloud the issue.

These moments also had a spiritual dimension to them. As a German woman named Claudia said to me, "I don't generally believe in God, but when I come here, I feel like I'm a bit closer to the heavens." And it's true, you do feel closer to the pearly gates here, at the rooftop of the world.

Our final days were spent walking through rhododendron forests. The red floral treetops, filled at times with black-faced and white-bearded Langur monkeys and fresh white snow on the ground, gave it an Asian Christmas feeling. And within a blink—18 days—we were finished. The quiet of the mountains replaced by honking horns, engines spewing out fumes, and the chatter of everyone trying to sell you something you don't need or want.

We were back in Kathmandu just in time for the "Holi" festival. The Holi festival's purpose is to welcome the upcoming rainy season after the long dry season. From my perspective, it looked more like an excuse to have a countrywide water balloon fight. Reunited with the Nolan family that I had met in Vietnam, we set out with Lucy and Jay in tow to see what was up with "Holi."

From windows and rooftops, buckets of water would come crashing down onto unsuspecting people below. It was like moving through an obstacle course where you could trust no one. Added to all of this were the "colors": red, orange, and yellow chalk dust that they would rub all over you and especially your face. It made for a very festive and colorful day, one that most people sat inside watching, safe and dry.

After "Holi," I said goodbye to Stephen; he was off for Paris again. I bunked up with a couple of Australians we met at the end of the trek, and began the preparation for my "dream trek" to the Everest base camp.

Kathmandu photographs   [57], page 117   [58], page 118

[1] Rua Manga Peak, (1,360 ft.), Rarotonga, Cook Islands

[2] Leleuvia Island, Fiji

[3] Sunset in Fiji

[4] My small white Nissan Sunny, New Zealand

[6] Green pastures, North Island, New Zealand

[5] Margaret Smith with homestead house, New Zealand

[7] Mount Ngauruhoe (7,500 ft.), North Island, New Zealand

[8] Me on Mount Ngauruhoe   photographer: Canadian

New Zealand is so beautiful!

[9] Canadian surprise on top of Mount Ngauruhoe, New Zealand

[10] Queen Charlotte Track, South Island, New Zealand

The fog freezes on the trees, creating a mystery feeling.

[11] Alexander, South Island, New Zealand

[12] Kea parrot on car, New Zealand

[13] Tasmanian farm pond, Australia

[15] Great Ocean Road of Southern Australia

[14] Tasmanian devil, Tasmania, Australia

The Tazzy devil
doesn't spin in circles!

[16] Yellow road sign, Wilson's Prom, Australia

*A chance to get up close
to the nature of Victoria.*

[17] Koala, Wilson's Prom, Australia

[18] Sydney Opera House, Sydney, Australia

The cows help with laundry in Murgen, Australia.

[19] Cows in clothesline, Queensland, Australia

[20] Diving on Great Barrier Reef, Port Douglas, Australia
photographer: unknown

[21] Car with fuel warning sign, outback Australia

[22] Ayers Rock or Uluru, Australia

[23] Henley-on-Todd Regatta Races in Alice Springs, Australia (I'm the last person in the boat on the right.)   photographer: unknown

[24] Ord River with reflection, Northern Territory, Australia

[25] Gibb River Road, Kimberly outback, Australia
photographer: unknown

[27] Guide holding frilled lizard, Northern Territory, Australia

[26] Aborigine cave art, Northern Territory, Australia

[28] Tree full of big bats, Northern Territory, Australia

[29] Kangaroos, Australia

[30] Rice field of Flores Island, Indonesia

[31] Woman riding moped, Bali, Indonesia

[32] Boat ride to Komodo Island, Indonesia
photographer: Neta Shermister

[33] Neta with Komodo dragon under our room, Komodo Island, Indonesia

[34] Komodo dragon, Komodo Island, Indonesia

*The bite of the Komodo dragon
is deadly!*

[35] Kelimutu Volcanic Lakes, Indonesia
photographer: Neta Shermister

[36] Mouth of Gunning Bromo Volcano, Java, Indonesia

[37] Kids playing in classroom, Moni, Flores Island, Indonesia

[38] Sindhu and me, Yogyakarta, Indonesia
photographer: Cynthia Webb

[39] The masks of Bali, Indonesia

[40] Borobudur Buddhist Temple, Yogyakarta, Indonesia

[41] Orangutan, Bukit Lawang, Indonesia

[42] Bangkok church at Christmas, Thailand

[43] Buddhist monk, Bangkok, Thailand

[44] Island beach, Thailand

[45] Mekong River, Laos

[46] Ho Chi Minh's Mausoleum, Hanoi, Vietnam

[47] Terraced rice fields, Sapa, Vietnam

[48] Vietnamese water taxi, Vietnam

[49] Village kids in schoolyard, Sapa, Vietnam

*Marble Mountain
is a Buddhist shrine with altars
inside a hollowed-out mountain.*

[50] Marble Mountain, Hoi An, Vietnam

[51] Roadside haircut, Nha Trang, Vietnam

*Most of the world
plants and harvests food
by hand.*

[52] Farmer in rice field with grave, Hue, Vietnam

[53] Shack on Mekong River, Vietnam

[54] Genocide memorial in the Killing Fields, Phnom Penh, Cambodia

A smile of hope.

[55] Young girl, Siem Reap, Cambodia

[56] Angkor Wat Temple, Cambodia

[57] Playing hide and go seek with village children, Annapurna Circuit, Nepal

photographer: Stephen Camron

[58] Prayer flags, Thorung La Pass (17,764 ft.), Nepal

[59] Mount Everest (29,035 ft.), Nepal

[60] Mount Ama Dablam (22,478 ft.), Nepal

[61] Glacier climbers, Mount Everest, Nepal

[62] Sherpa carrying heavy load, Nepal

Nepal
is a very poor country.

[63] Kathmandu City, Nepal

[64] Boy sleeping, Kathmandu City, Nepal

[65] Birthplace of Buddha, Lumbini, Nepal
photographer: unknown

*The atmosphere
was quiet and peaceful,
just what you want a sacred location to be.*

*Thousands of Hindu people
cleansing the soul.*

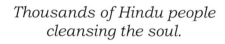

[66] Ganga River, Varanasi, India

[67] Morning prayer, Varanasi, India

[68] Sadhu (holy man), India

[69] Beautiful women of India

[70] Floating on the Ganga, Varanasi, India
photographer: unknown

[71] Teaching English to Tibetians, McLeodganj, India   photographer: unknown

[72] Teaching the Hokie Pokie, Lamayaru, India

photographer: Alessandra

[73] Young girl, Ladakh, India

*Those with so little
have so much
inside.*

[74] Narrow road of Ladakh, India

[75] Young smiles, Zanskar Trek, Ladakh, India

[76] Mountain pass, Zanskar Trek, Ladakh, India

photographer: Jan Knaapen

[77] Herding goats, Zanskar Trek, Ladakh, India

[78] Srinagar, Kashmir Valley, India

[79] The Golden Temple, Amritsar, India
photographer: unknown

[80] Dubai, UAE (United Arab Emirates)

[81] Blue Mosque, Istanbul, Turkey

[82] Mosaic of Jesus, Aya Sofya, Turkey

[83] Trojan horse, Troy, Turkey
photographer: unknown

eeeehhhaaaaa!!!

[84] Paragliding, Fethiye, Turkey
photographer: unknown

[85] Houses in stone, Cappadocia, Turkey

[86] Mount Ararat at sunset, Dogubayzit, Turkey

The
Kurdish people
were warm and friendly.

[87] Kurdish kid, Tatvan, Turkey

[88] Kurdish family - 10 children, Tatvan, Turkey

[89] Whirling dervishes, Konya, Turkey

[90] Young Islamic girl at border, Syria

[91] Me dressed as an Arab, Aleppo, Syria
photographer: unknown

[92] Roman ruins in desert, Palmyra, Syria

[93] Bedouin girl outside tent, Syria

[94] Umayyad Mosque, Damascus, Syria

[96] Woman making tea in the desert, Wadi Rum, Jordan

[95] Petra ruins, Jordan

[97] Desert campsite, Wadi Rum, Jordan

[98] Western Wall, Jerusalem, Israel

[99] Dome of the Rock, Jerusalem, Israel

[101] Birthplace of Jesus, Bethlehem, Palestinian Territories

[100] Orthodox Jews, Jerusalem, Israel

[102] Boy floating in the Dead Sea, Israel

[103] Sunset at Tel Aviv, Israel

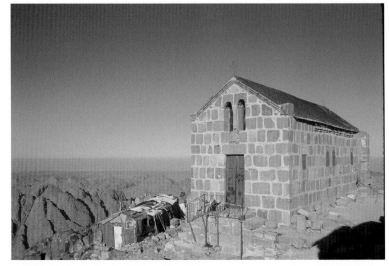

[104] Chapel on top of Mount Sinai, Egypt

*Seeing
the pyramids
was a dream come true.*

[105] Pyramid, Giza, Egypt

[106] Me and Sphinx, Giza, Egypt
photographer: unknown

[107] Flukas on the Nile River, Egypt

[108] Me on Nile fluka sailboat, Nile River, Egypt
photographer: unknown

[109] Young Egyptian girl, Egypt

[110] Hama woman, Jinka, Ethiopia

[111] Man walking with poles, Ethiopia

[112] Village in the bush, Ethiopia

[113] Me on the bus with cement workers, Ethiopia
photographer: unknown

[114] Woman on road with baby, Kenya

[115] Truck stuck in the mud, Kenya

[116] Flamingos on lake, Lake Nakuru, Kenya

[117] Masai Village kids, Masai Mara, Kenya

[118] Masai boy jumping, Kenya

[119] The Masai in line to vote, Kenya

[120] Election day celebration, Nairobi, Kenya

[121] Safari sunrise in the trees, Serengeti, Tanzania

[122] Zebras, Ngorongoro Crater, Tanzania

[123] Lions on grass, Ngorongoro Crater, Tanzania

[124] Elephants in the Serengeti, Tanzania

[125] Safari truck, Serengeti, Tanzania

[126] Victoria Falls, Livingstone, Zambia

Whitewater rafting with crocodiles.

[127] Rafting the Zambezi, Zambia
photographer: unknown

[128] Flight over Victoria Falls, Zambia
photographer: remote control

Hanging on for dear life.

[129] Fur seals on the beach, Cape Cross, Namibia

[130] Sand dunes quad ride, Swakopmund, Namibia

[131] Giraffes in the road, Namibia

[132] Soussusvlei Desert, Namibia

[134] Me with the penguins, South Africa
photographer: Alex

[133] Township kid, Capetown, South Africa

[135] Watching the sunset above Capetown, Lion's Head,
South Africa   photographer: unknown

[136] Denmark party, Arhus, Denmark
photographer: timer

Good friends are priceless.

[137] Rose of Paris, France

[138] Eiffel Tower, Paris, France

Lower Manhattan 1970

[139] Prayer-filled billboard at Ground Zero, New York City, New York USA

[140] Australian tombstone, outback Australia

Entry Twenty-seven: The dream comes true

A long time ago someone asked if I would like to climb Everest. I said no, for reasons already stated. But I *did* say that I would love to go to the base camp someday. So off I went, alone this time, to fulfill a dream that was planted a long time ago.

As I prepared one morning in Kathmandu for my trek, I was startled by a large blast. I looked to one of my Aussie roomates and quietly said, "That was no firecracker."

The next day the news revealed a bomb had exploded on a bridge a few blocks away. Twenty-four people were injured by the blast that had been set off by the Maoists. My safe little haven of Kathmandu was becoming less safe.

In better shape than I'd been a month before, at 7 AM one morning I climbed into a twin engine prop plane that was to fly me to Lukla, my starting and ending point for the trek. The plane, stuffed with people and baggage, climbed out of the Kathmandu Valley and flew over river valleys and mountains peaks covered with snow.

As I peered out the plane's window, my thoughts drifted like the clouds just outside. I wondered about life in the small houses and villages below. What was life like there with no roads, just paths connecting them to the outside world? What did the villagers think about? Did they ever lie on the ground, look up to the sky and wonder who was in these planes flying by, as I did when I was a child in Nebraska? Or were they busier wondering, "How will I feed my children?" and "Will the Maoists spare my house?" I suspected both.

Landing in Lukla, one literally drops out of the sky. The runway is short, slanted uphill to take advantage of gravity, and comes to a mountainside-abrupt stop. The other end is a drop off a cliff. So, it's important to get it right. I sat up front. This allowed me to look over the shoulders of the pilots and watch the action as it happened.

After landing, I immediately set off. Eager to be on my way, and ready for a little solitude, I walked for seven hours to Namche Bazaar. Alone for most of the day, I found the trek quiet and invigorating, but problems were brewing in my stomach. I'd eaten something bad, and rumblings broke the otherwise silent air. Either I have a sensitive stomach or bad luck, but once again I found myself on pilgrimages to the small room all too often.

Spending an extra night in Namche to get better, one evening I awoke with a full bladder. I winced at the thought of leaving my warm sleeping bag and going down to the basement on the other side of the building. I opted for plan B. I stood on my bed, opened the window from my second floor room, poked out my head to scan the curfewed empty main street and peed. The moon shone down on me in full. It lit up the night, and the only sound was a stream of water hitting a blue plastic tarp used as an overhanging roof top. I climbed back into my still warm sleeping bag feeling pleased with my own cleverness, and fell back asleep.

Jimmy Carter once stayed in this lodge back in 1985 when he climbed up to the base camp. On the wall was a plaque that said, "President Carter once slept here," along with a photo of him on the wall of the dining room. I found the fact pretty cool, and he gained my respect for having the gumption to do it. This trek is filled with history, which is part of its draw. In a small way you get to feel and be a tiny part of the Everest mystique. Not just observing, but also doing, is a rare experience.

The next few days moved slowly. I walked with Chris, a German acquaintance, for a couple of days. Since he kept a slow pace, I ventured on ahead and ended up meeting a group of expatriates from England. I spent the remainder of my trek with them. They had come from all over and met up in Nepal: Chris from Dubi, Chris from Indonesia, Ian from Indonesia, and JJ from Singapore, along with Tilak the guide. I became the token American. They provided great company and interesting conversations, all very successful in the world. I provided comic relief.

One evening as we gained altitude, I awoke with a mild case of AMS (altitude mountain sickness). The room was spinning, and it was way too cold to try and stick my leg out of my sleeping bag to try and stop it. Eventually, I slowly put on my clothes and walked outside for a bathroom break. This brought some relief. Then, as I started to fall back asleep, my breathing would stop momentarily, waking me up, short of breath and afraid to fall back to sleep. For hours I laid there, staring at the ceiling, half propped up to stop the spinning and half hoping someone else might wake up and want to go to a lower altitude, allowing me to join them. But no one did. I slowly slipped back to sleep and awoke the next morning a bit tired, but feeling much better.

The next day brought us to the highest guesthouse of the trek, Gorak Sherp. We arrived in the late morning. My trekking companions had decided to go on to the Everest base camp. I decided to rest and climb Kala Pattar, taking my chances to view Everest at sunset. The rock knoll offers a view of Everest and the surrounding mountains and valleys.

Most people climb up Kala Pattar first thing in the morning. It's a smart plan, given that it is almost always clear in the morning, almost guaranteeing a clear view, unlike the evening which generally clouds up every night. The trek up Kala Pattar took two to three hours from Gorak Sherp. So at 2:30 PM, I set off alone, with every piece of warm clothing I had in my backpack, along with my flashlight. My secret plan was to watch the sunset's rays beam onto Mt. Everest. The chances for a clear view were slim, but the sun would be at my back in the evening, offering the best angle for photos. In my mind, the risk was worth taking.

The other risk, of course, was darkness. Slowly I worked my way up Kala Pattar. The clouds started building up at the end of the long valley. Completely alone, I savored every step like a child enjoying his favorite piece of candy after a dinner of liver and onions. As I climbed higher, Everest crept into more and more of the view. As it grew, so did the deep well of my emotions.

From time to time I had to stop and allow the tears to come; the tears of gratitude, of never giving up on my long-held dream. Tears of happiness and humility fell as I felt the presence of the Divine. It was as if God had led me on this long journey just so we could have this moment to dance together, as the gods of the Himalayan Mountains surrounded us and cheered us on. The transformation of dream into reality, of someday into now, is a powerful mark in time, both fleeting and intangible. It is the fulfillment of Providence, which can be experienced only in the heart of those who are willing to dare. The magic of knowing, of being aware that this moment was planned before you were born, and you somehow overcame all the potential distractions, and followed the purest place in your heart, which allowed it to bloom in full glory.

And so we danced all the way to the top of Kala Pattar. At the top, a small group of trekkers had gathered to take in the incredible view of Everest and the surrounding mountains. It was cool and breezy. The clouds from the lower valley were now making their way up the mountainsides. Soon, waves of clouds were passing over us, at times obscuring the view. People began leaving, and before long it was just myself and John from Australia.

Together we walked to the base camp, as they included me for a brief moment in their expedition. We arrived to find a part of the glacier covered with colorful tents strung about. Each expedition had its area staked out. After finding theirs, they invited me in for coffee. I sat around the table with them, listening to stories, introducing myself to the other members of the climbing team. This was the closest I was ever going to get to being a part of an Everest climb, and I was totally enjoying it!

After two hours of visiting and looking around, I bid them farewell and wished my luck onto them: "I am a lucky, lucky man, and I wish that onto you." They liked that.

I had yet another seven hours of trekking to do to reach the meeting place agreed upon. It was time to get moving. Tracing back over my steps, with the final views of Everest, I said goodbye, blew a kiss from my heart and moved down the valley. In the evening the trail was very empty, as most people had already arrived at their destinations. So once again it was just me for several hours. The last two hours I followed a yak team, trusting them as my guide. With darkness closing in fast, I stumbled into the lodge to hear the words, "We were just talking about you. We didn't think you were going to make it."

The rest of the way down was spent trying to catch the Brits. They were moving fast, and I was ready to finish, so it worked well as a carrot to keep me moving. Back in Kathmandu, we met for dinner one evening to celebrate. That evening they presented me with my own official team member shirt. I was quite touched by that, and appreciated their kindness. Again it was time to say goodbye—but I had four new friends.

While having a philosophical conversation with someone who asked about what I do, I responded, "This. This is my life right now. I travel. It's not a vacation, or long holiday, it's my life. And when this chapter is finished, I will start the next chapter of my life.

"I'm a lucky man who gets to have a chapter in his life of a long journey, to learn more about the world than sound bites of only bad things."

And so my life continued. I was stuck in Kathmandu for days waiting for a package in the middle of a Maoist strike. All part of travel. While filling in time, I snuck in a two-day whitewater rafting trip. It was a blast and reminded me of how much I enjoy floating on the rivers and the adventure that brings. I also made friends with a Mr. Stokes from London, a writer for a House of Parliament member. We swapped political stories and discussed philosophical issues into the wee hours over beers.

One of the tactics the Maoists would use against the sitting government of Nepal was to call a countrywide strike. They would declare certain dates as a strike period and almost all business would come to a standstill. The taxis who were willing to dare and work in spite of the strike would tape paper over there license plates so they couldn't be traced. Some shops would pull the doors down three-quarters of the way, allowing people to bend over and crawl in, while at the same time enabling them to lock up quickly if needed.

As a traveler, this pretty much sucked. The buses would stop moving, and it would limit your movement to areas close to where you were staying. During one of these strike days, I decided to rent a small motorcycle. A friend of mine from Israel, Moran, had suggested we go exploring on our own. Thinking this was a great idea, I procured a nice motorbike and away we went with her riding on the back. As we rode through the mostly empty and quiet city, around a corner from behind, a taxi came zipping into us, sending us crashing onto the street.

Scraped up and beat up, we laid on the ground as a crowd gathered around looking down at us. Soon the police arrived, and we were being carried off to a nearby emergency hospital. The taxi driver had stopped and followed us into the hospital, along with the crowd and police. I remembered reading somewhere that when you have an accident in a poor country, it doesn't matter whose fault it is, those with the money have to pay. There were several conversations going on around us, of which I understood not one word.

My first concern was Moran. It was her first ride on a motorcycle, and most likely her last. She seemed to be okay. Nothing was broken—only some real good cuts and scratches. My right leg was another matter.

When I hit the ground, I hit the space right below my kneecap, the part they tap to check your reflexes. The sensitive spot was jammed into a chrome pipe that surrounded the engine. It was painful, and soon began to swell, which made it difficult to walk. The nurse wanted to x-ray my leg. I suggested that it was all right, more out of fear of causing undesired focus on the problem. In addition to that, I looked around the place thinking to myself, "I've seen better veterinarian clinics than what this place looks like. Yikes!"

After a while one of the policemen approached and asked me if it would be all right for him to give the taxi driver's license back to him. Surprised that he would ask me such a question, I said that would be fine, it was an accident. When the bill was totaled and about to be delivered to me, the policeman took it from the nurse and gave it to the taxi driver, who accepted it with a look of disgust.

I was never once asked what happened. Apparently there were enough witnesses around to give him the story, or enough of a story to let us go. My passenger was still shaken up, so I asked the police to give her a ride home, which they happily agreed to. Then I hobbled back to my motorbike, straightened the handlebars as best I could, took some dirt to rub over the scratches and hopped back on. Slowly and cautiously I rode it back across town to the place where I rented it from and told them I had changed my mind for the day and decided to stay home. I hopped off and handed them the bike and with my best effort, tried not to limp as I walked away.

I spent most of the next week in bed icing my leg, praying it would heal and reading everything I could get my hands on. I even read the manual to my camera twice! Happy to be alive, I rested, extended my visa and prepared myself for India.

Kathmandu is a large city that has a great deal of visible poverty. But I never felt unsafe, and found most people to be humble and kind.

The dream comes true photographs   [59], page 119   [60], page 120   [61], page 121
                                            [62], page 121   [63], page 122   [64], page 122

Entry Twenty-eight: Side trip to Lumbini

When the time came for me to leave Kathmandu, I was anxious to be on my way. My extra time there gave my body a chance to rest, to read several books and to learn more about my complex camera. (You'd think after a year I would know everything about it.) It was a mini-computer and all the buttons were related to each other in so many ways, it got tricky. The refresher course was good!

Jumping onto the bus at 7 AM, I began my 12-hour ride. The bus was crammed full of Nepalis. The only other westerners were a New Zealand couple heading for the same place as myself: Lumbini, the birthplace of Buddha.

At one point on the journey, the passenger sitting next to me began to lean over towards the window. He was getting sick. The next thing I knew, he was on my lap, puking out the window. I did everything I could to pull myself to his seat in a crowded bus where I could barely move. Obviously, I let him have the window seat for the rest of the trip.

Occasionally we would have to stop at a police checkpoint. Some of these checkpoints would take an hour to get through. At one of these stops, I hopped out for a stretch and a brief walk. Walking along the roadside, I noticed that every bus had the streaks similar to the ones near the window seat I'd just given up. I guess my ridemate wasn't the only one getting sick.

Without much warning, it was announced that we were at Lumbini. We jumped off the bus and got a cycle-rickshaw to our hotel. About five minutes into that ride, I realized that I had left my walking stick and my most precious hat on the bus. In a moment of panic, I jumped off the bike, spied the bus, and turned the bike around, explaining what I had done.

The driver was pedaling as fast as he could. Still, we watched as the bus pulled away, leaving us behind. Soon we came to a motorbike heading towards us. We flagged him down, and I jumped on the back of his bike, leaving my large pack with the rickshaw driver. The motorbike rider spoke no English, so the rickshaw driver explained to him what happened, and we were off chasing the bus down the road.

Dodging cows and bicycles and people, we chased down the bus—so we thought. It was the wrong one, so we kept going. My mind started to wander. If I had known that the bus I was looking for wasn't the first bus I saw, I probably would have let it go. But there I was on the back of a motorbike with someone who didn't speak English, chasing a bus nowhere in sight. On top of that, I'd left my large pack, full of clothes, sleeping bag, some money—you get the picture—with someone whose first name I didn't even know. In addition, darkness was falling. For the next 30 minutes we just kept weaving our way through people and cows. Then finally in the distance, I spotted the taillights of a bus.

We caught up with them as they stopped to let off a passenger in the middle of nowhere. Honking and flashing our light, they waited for us. I hopped off the bike, stepped onto the bus and heard, "Dean, you're back!" from some of the passengers I had met. I walked to my seat and sure enough, up above in the luggage rack were my hat and walking stick. I couldn't believe it. We had found the bus. Saying goodbye for a second time to my bus mates, I hopped on the back of the motorbike and headed back to Lumbini. Along the way I tried to explain to my driver that this was no ordinary hat or everyday stick, to justify our crazy ride.

By now it was completely dark. The night air was full of bugs, which seemed to be magnetically drawn to our faces. I was jubilant to have my hat back. At the same time, I was half-wondering if I'd ever see my backpack again. My driver was still wondering what made that hat so important. (My hat was the first thing I acquired when I made the decision to take my journey. You know that, but to this day I'm not sure that poor driver ever caught on.)

We came to the intersection where the bus had dropped us off, just a crossroads in the countryside with a few roadside shops. We looked around for the cycle rickshaw driver. At first, we couldn't find him. Then from one of the roadside cafes I heard a "Hey, mister!" There he was waiting for me with my pack. Surveying my pack quickly, I could see all the locks were still in place; all my stuff was there!

We sat down and I bought three Cokes to celebrate. We had a few laughs, and I paid the drivers something for their time. We then set off, once again intact, for the hotel. Outside the hotel where he dropped me off, there was a party to celebrate a wedding announcement. There was a large tent serving food and a band playing some kind of music.

I checked into my hotel and went to take a peek at what was going on. As I was watching, one of the Nepali men who was dancing came over and pulled me into the circle of celebrants. We started dancing! This was big entertainment; a large crowd soon gathered around to watch. Even with my bad leg it was good to dance. I was so happy to have found my things and dancing was what I felt like doing.

Afterwards they pulled me into the tent and stuffed me with food. Everyone came by to shake my hand and tell me that I was a good dancer. I gave my congratulations to the future groom and bid them all goodnight.

It was time to collapse into bed after a very long day. The next morning brought with it the heat of the coming day. Grabbing my daypack, I set out to discover the Sacred Garden, the birthplace of Buddha. I walked slowly with my walking stick in hand. The empty road into the park was such a contrast to the busy streets of Kathmandu; the atmosphere was quiet and peaceful, just what you want a sacred location to be.

Next to the park garden was the pond where Maya Devi took a bath right before giving birth to Buddha. It was situated near a large Bodi tree covered with prayer flags. In the trunk of the tree, a shrine had been built honoring this sacred site. Sitting under the shade of the Bodi tree, I closed my eyes and enjoyed the breeze that swept across my perspiring wet skin. When I finished resting and thinking, I cut off a small lock of hair and left it as my devotional offering of gratitude to this special place.

Then I walked down to the pond, knelt down, and put my hand into the water to feel the coolness. I could sense how the water brought the same refreshing coolness to Maya Devi, a long time ago. With this, my time in Nepal came to an end.

I will always love Nepal with its breathtaking beauty, kind people and smiling children. But India was waiting for me.

Side trip to Lumbini photograph   [65], page 123

Entry Twenty-nine: Thank you, India

Crossing the border into India was like walking down the main street of a busy small town. Eventually I came to the immigration office, which was a desk sitting under the overhang of an ordinary building. If I hadn't been paying close attention, I could have easily missed it. With an open border between Nepal and India, the only people who stop are travelers like myself. Climbing onto a crowded bus (do you sense a pattern here?), I sardined my way to Gorakpur and caught a night train to Varanasi.

Varanasi is a major holy site for the Hindu religion. According to their belief, a bath in the Ganges River at this place has special powers to purify the soul. Thus it is an important pilgrimage destination for all Hindus. In the early morning light as the sun rises, Hindus line the bank of the Mother Ganges, performing the ritual bathing. It is a sight like no other, with the red glow of the morning sun shining on thousands of bathers.

With the heat of the day having reached 105 degrees and getting hotter, I decided to keep my stay short. My next destination point was Bodngaya, the holiest of places for Buddhism. Bodngaya is the location where Buddha sat under the tree and gained enlightenment. It is a relatively small place filled with temples built by various countries where Buddhism is a major religion. After performing my ongoing ritual of finding a bed, I rented a bike and set out to find the temple. Soon I found myself sitting under the Bodi tree where Buddha once sat, hoping that a little enlightenment might rub off on me. I could only hope.

After a brief and hot stay, I headed for the train station and began my 30-hour train ride to Rishikesh, a one-time Guru hangout visited by the Beatles. It was a very long ride. No air-conditioned compartments were available so, crammed into an upper bunk, I hunkered down for the long ride north in search of cooler weather. Hour after hour, the scenery was open, dry fields occasionally broken up with groves of trees.

At one point, I noticed several wild peacocks walking through the fields. The train stopped often—at every town, it seemed like. Sometimes I would hop down from my bed and walk to the end of the railcar. I opened the door and watched the countryside go by, enjoying the breeze.

The locals always wanted to talk with me, a traveler. The conversations were nice but still, there were times when I just wanted to sit and read or be quiet. People rarely gave me that space. Overall, the people were lovely and a joy to be around.

After 30 hours of riding, someone could have stuck a fork in me—I was well done.

After a brief stay in Rishikesh, I set out for Gangotri. Gangotri is where the road ends and the trail begins for Gaumukh, the home of the headwaters of the Ganges River. Gaumukh translates into "the mouth of the cow." The Ganges is a "mother god" for the Hindus, a god in liquid form that possesses the ability to cleanse your soul when you take a bath. The Ganges gives life to all of India through the gift of water and in the creation of all things.

A seed was planted in me some time ago to go trekking to the headwaters of the Ganges. This was the day that seed sprouted and came to life. Just getting to Gangotri was a long ride (so what's new?). It was 12 hours from Rishikesh, much of it along a single lane road that hugged the cliffs of the steep valley. Halfway there, I switched to a jeep because the buses had stopped running for the day.

It was during my jeep ride that I met Yogi Shivnath. Yogi was from Bombay, but was constantly traveling to sacred places throughout India. At 75 years of age, he was in remarkably good shape—a testament to his last 40 years of practicing spiritual Yoga. Our conversation on the jeep was intriguing and welcome, because it went beyond "Where are you from," "What do you do," "Are you married," and "Why not?" Yogi spoke good English. He was very educated and had been a successful businessman, traveling abroad.

When we arrived in Gangotri, Yogi invited me to share a room with him. I accepted his invitation. After my long journey, I just wanted a bed. Within minutes of climbing into bed, I was asleep. The next thing I recall was hearing Yogi's voice, "Wake up, wake up, it's time to meditate!"

At 5 AM, the first thing on my mind was it's time to sleep or pee. However, up I sat, legs crossed, and followed him as he led me through a two-hour meditation. It was good and I found it refreshing for both my body and spirit. After a bite of breakfast, I bid him farewell and made plans to see him after my trek to Gaumukh.

It felt so good to be back in the cool air of the mountains after the sweltering heat of the Indian plains. Stunning and beautiful as ever, the Himalayan Mountains once again welcomed me into their abode. The trail was filled with pilgrims heading for the same place. Families, Sadhus (holy men), people from all walks of life; some carried by mules, others carried by people like some kind of royalty. Most Hindus, poor and wealthy alike, come to this place once in their lifetime.

When I reached Bhojbasa, I discovered that my guidebook was wrong about available lodging. I was faced with finding a place to stay. I ended up in the ashram with all the pilgrims, which meant I had to share floor space with a boatload of other people. As long as I was out of the elements for the night, I was happy.

My floormates spoke little English, but that didn't stop them from having a conversation with me. Most of the time I just smiled, and cocked my head to the side like a puppy does when watching something it doesn't understand. I awoke in the middle of the night to go to the bathroom (outside). I opened the door and was greeted by falling snow. By the time I got up we had four inches on the ground, covering everything. The Indians were like small children, underdressed, playing in the snow. For them, snow is a novel thing that is rarely experienced.

Slipping on my boots and stuffing things back into my backpack, I started my day's journey—much to the amazement of my floormates who were huddled together under the covers. The sky was clear and blue, and the trail was empty. I took advantage of the empty trail and set off for Gaumuhk, alone in the white snow and quiet.

As I trekked up I was surrounded by towering peaks, and noted a glacier winding down a valley to come to an abrupt stop. From underneath this glacier a river appeared: Gaumuhk, the start of the amazing Mother Ganga. A brown, milky water, full of nutrients and rich in minerals, it begins its race across India toward the ocean.

I walked down to the riverside, knelt down and paid my respects to the mighty Ganges. The water was icy cold. I heard the rumble of boulders, once prisoners in ice, tumbling down, hidden in the milky waters. Not a safe place to swim. They call this Ganga music. After one last silent moment, I began the long trek back to Gangotri.

Thank you, India photographs   [66], page 124   [67], page 124   [68], page 125
    [69], page 125   [70], page 125

Entry Thirty: Gaumukh, the mouth

The snow had melted and the trail was once again filled with Hindu pilgrims on their once-in-a-lifetime journey. After eight hours, I walked back into Gangotri and plopped down at the same teahouse where I'd started my journey.

No sooner had I finished my cup of tea when Yogi appeared, saying, "Let's go for a walk." Although my body was thinking more about a warm shower and a soft bed, I agreed.

Yogi looked like you would imagine a yogi to look like: he had a white beard, and was dressed in an orange robe with a red shawl. As we walked, he said, "Look at those trees. On the branches of those trees there are millions of yogis living, but you can't see them unless your third eye is open. Mine once was, but now it's closed for some reason.

"They spoke to me one time. They live here in this sacred place next to the Ganges. Like a million bright lights shining on, they shine on all who come here."

After a few moments of silence, I asked him, "Yogi, why is it when I'm in nature my spirit seems to go 'aaaaahhhhh'—a peacefulness settles over me?" He responded, "That is because it is recognizing all of these places. Over the millions of years, as your spirit has passed through here, it has left its imprint on all the rocks, the trees, and all the ageless things of this world. Your spirit recognizes these imprints it once left, which helps it feel at ease and at home."

Nice thought. Yogi was full of information; at times, too much, which could make my head spin and give me a headache. The Hindu religion is so old and such a conglomerate of various practices and rituals that it can easily become overwhelming for me. I do appreciate the diversity, richness, and the depth of devotion practiced by the Hindus. As for me, I just have a deep love for God, and the Hindus are included within that.

Yogi was appreciating our time together as much as I was, but the time came for me to leave. Without me telling him that I was leaving in the morning, at the end of our last walk together he turned away towards his room saying, "All the best to you," and disappeared down the stairs.

In the morning I hopped onto the bus and began heading towards Dharmashala, home of the Dalai Lama.

My journey to Dharmashala took me back through Rishikesh and the heat. I stayed long enough to take my bath in the Ganges River, not wanting to miss out on its soul-cleansing qualities. (In addition, by the time the water reached here, it was a bit warmer.) A very old man led me through the ritual as a small crowd gathered. They watched in amazement, I imagine, mostly due to the look on my face in the freezing waters.

I caught a train in Haridwar and headed north, once again packed in with others like sardines. We slowly made our way to Panthankot. In Panthankot I jumped onto a bus and arrived in Dharmashala some 24 hours later.

Within a couple of days I started teaching English to Tibetan refugees, and made a temporary home for myself. It was an interesting time to be there. Tensions between India and Pakistan were on the world stage. Information could be a little sketchy, but everything was very calm. I looked at it very closely: Was the calm a denial of what was happening or is the fear an overreaction?

News generally comes in the form of bad news, the gaps of accurate and true information left to be filled in by our imaginations. This is generally tilted towards the worse, which leads to more fear and panic. I was determined to stay until my internal readings changed, in which case I'd leave without question.

It is a delicate walk that I take seriously and with diligence. More than anything I trust my heart, to what and where it will lead me.

After listening to His Holiness the Dalai Lama speak the next day, I found myself moved by his presence, his wisdom, gentleness, and compassion. As he left the presentation, I was close enough to reach out and touch him. For a brief moment we exchanged smiles. His eyes were filled with light, as well as his smile. It was amazing, and my wish to feel his presence came true. He truly is a special man, and embodies the purest qualities that he talks about.

His talk also stirred me up inside (not a bad thing), and left me asking questions of myself. He talked about how precious life is, that we should not waste it. So then, I had to ask myself, was I wasting my life on the current traveling? Or, would to continue traveling be wasting my life, given that I'd already had so many learning and growing experiences?

At that point I didn't know the answer—or maybe I did—but it was good to be engaged in such questions. It also led to other questions: "What is the best use of this life? How can I help relieve the needless suffering of others, to contribute to the growth and well-being of society? If I weren't traveling, learning about the world and myself, then what would I be doing?"

These were crucial and hard questions that I constantly struggled with on that day, and each day of the journey since. The answers I seek sincerely, and trust they will come. It is my responsibility to recognize them when they do come! Am I running away, or am I running towards something? Maybe both. I seek personal answers to questions that have been asked as long as questions have been asked. I do know that doing the same thing, hoping to find different answers, was not going to bring me what I'm searching for.

Ultimately it is a question that only I can answer for myself. Even with all the outside information coming to me, it is to my counsel within that I go to find my personal answers, and trust my own destiny will unfold before me.

So my journey continued.

Gaumukh, the mouth photograph   [71], page 126

Entry Thirty-one: Long journeys, both in & out

I finished my ten-day Vipassana meditation course: ten days of silence, hours of quietness, hours of mind torture, hours of peace, and hours of a sore butt.

I loved it all. The technique was first taught by Siddhartha Gautama Buddha 2,500 years ago. Its lasting effectiveness is a testament to its purity and usefulness. Was it easy? No. Was it simple? Yes. I won't bore you with the details of the technique or how it works. Besides, it must be experienced to be understood. But here's the short version: We sat with our eyes closed eight hours a day, with a few short breaks throughout the day.

As we sat there in long rows on top of neatly arranged pillows, it brought to me an image of a hen house. My mind wandered from time to time in our quest for dharma (truth). At one point, I got the idea of drawing some egg-shaped pieces of paper, and writing "Dharma Egg" on them. Toward the end of the course, I quietly slipped the papers onto the pillows of a few people I had gotten to know earlier, and sat there in silence as they entered the room.

The fellow next to me came in first and sat down and started giggling. I struggled not to burst out laughing. I had to bite my thumb to keep a roaring laugh from erupting as the others discovered their eggs and fought back their laughter. One poor fellow, someone from Europe, missed the joke and thought it was a note from the teacher to work harder. We both had a good laugh over that.

The room that held 84 of us (plus assistants) was always in pure silence. It was a great environment in which to do the internal work Vipassana required. The room had a special feeling or presence to it, like a sanctuary. So imagine the impact of one participant that started to snore loud enough to rattle the windows. After a little quiet laughter, and a dirty look from one of the staff members, he was gently tapped on the shoulder and awakened.

One of my roommates made up for the daylong silence by talking all night long in his sleep. In the end we laughed about it. It was like having bedtime stories all night long.

The teachings were excellent; the stories were informative and interesting. I learned much about Buddhism and Buddha, and felt greater clarity about something that was a little confusing to me. A saint I'm not, and that was clear to me as the first words that I spoke to a staff member after 5 days of not speaking one word were, "I'm constipated." (I don't think that's going to make any of the holy books, but we all have to start somewhere.)

My time in Dharmsala was fruitful and nourishing for body, mind and spirit. My time spent teaching English to Tibetan refugees was touching. This is a wonderful culture—kind, caring and with a great sense of humor.

One student insisted I come home with him one evening to have dinner. We sat around a table that was off to one side in his one-room house. Plastic covered the ceiling to help keep the rain out. His wife cooked us dinner and they told me their story.

They spent a month walking through the mountains to escape from the Chinese in Tibet. He had farmed on the high plateau of Tibet, and spoke lovingly of the horses that helped him work the land. I shared their heartbreak over the children they had to leave behind. They shared so much with me, freely, even though they had so little. They didn't ask for anything; they were just happy to enjoy my company.

Such grace and humility was very special to be around. It seemed to mark this place.

Entry Thirty-two: Way up north

The road from Manali to Leh is two days of breathtaking, underwear-changing beauty. At times the road is literally carved out of the side of sheer cliffs.

This wouldn't be such a big deal if it were two lanes instead of one. Meeting other vehicles was always an event, one that often had me closing my eyes. Along the way I couldn't help but take notice of remnants of vehicles at the bottom of gorges and on cliff sides that hadn't fared so well. God was smiling on me these days; we made it with only one broken spring. Repairmen ended up using rope to tie it together. I still haven't figured out how that ever worked.

The road cut across the Himalayan range and took me north to the high altitude area of Leh Ladakh (3,500 meters) where little, if any, of the monsoon rains ever reached. These high-desert mountains, with their green veins of vegetation nurtured by the snow and glacial melt, were an incredible sight. There was such a great contrast: either there was water and green, or else brown, barren land that reminded one of the moon. It was this distinct difference that gave one the impression, when one was in a green place, of an oasis or the Garden of Eden.

The second day of that journey we started at 2 AM, and didn't stop until 1 AM the next morning. That was how I spent my 40th birthday: bouncing down the road, soaking up the views, and teaching English to Tibetan nuns with shaved heads. It was the longest birthday I've ever had, and one of the most unassuming. It was a good way to bring in 40.

After I found my room and took a much-needed shower, I set off to find some people I had met earlier in Manali. We had talked about exploring together, and I was interested in going with them. As it turned out, they had hired a jeep and invited me to come along with them for the next two days to explore some of the countryside. Perfect!

The next morning we set off: Sunita from India (who lives in the U.S.), Alessandra from Switzerland, Massimo from Italy and me. They were all my age, more or less, and it was fun to go exploring with a like-minded small group. They also loved to take photos, and with a hired jeep we could stop whenever we wanted. Such a luxury you forfeit when you ride on the bus.

When we arrived in the village where we were to spend the night, we stopped at a roadside cafe to eat. Across from the cafe was a public school with two classrooms of small children. Venturing over there, I soon found myself in front of a classroom teaching English. Before too long the entire school was in the schoolyard in circle formation doing the Hokey Pokey. The innocent laughter of children was such a rich reward; I was lucky to have been given such a vast experience of these moments.

Back in Leh I made a decision to embark on the Zanskar Trek, a demanding ten-day journey that included seven mountain passes which peaked at over 4,500 meters. Checking around Leh, all of the trekking agencies wanted anywhere from $30 to $55 a day for a guided trek. This was way out of my $10-a-day budget. So after some checking around, I discovered one could go to the trekking route and find much cheaper options. With my mind set on finding a "pony man" in Padum, I figured I'd fly by the seat of my pants.

A day before leaving, I met a man called Tundup at the Dalai Lama's birthday festival held in Leh. Tundup spoke a little English and said he was a pony man and was interested in coming with me on my trek. So the next day we both set off on the two-day journey heading for Padum.

It was at this point that I broke the travelers' rule and sat in the very last row of the bus (the only seat left). For two days I spent more time in the air than on my seat, as we traveled over some of the worst roads in the region. In addition, the bus was packed to the gills with luggage. The middle isle was stacked so high with boxes and bags that it towered above the heads of the passengers sitting in the seats next to it. This meant we had to crawl over the tops of things, like some kind of obstacle course, to get to our seats.

As we bounced down the dry, dirt road, the dust got so thick I could hardly breathe. My handkerchief slowly turned from blue to brown as I held it over my mouth to try to breathe. Along the route there were several police checkpoints that required me to escape from my small hole and show my passport to the officials. I resorted to crawling in and out of the window, which was far easier than crawling through the bus.

The road was a mere dirt track that took us over high mountain passes, alongside huge glaciers, and past high mountain pastures dotted with the tents of nomadic herdsmen and their families. What I could see from my little hole was beautiful. Eventually we made it to Padum, where I made plans to meet Tundup in his home village of Pishu in two days. We'd continue the trek together from there.

On the bus I had met some teachers from a nearby village. The village happened to be on my trek. The teachers invited me to visit the school and teach for a day. After a recovery night in a hotel in Padum, I set off for the Marpaling Model School in Thongday. I got there a little late; the two-hour walk was actually four hours. The school operates on donations mainly from Europe; they have 70 students and are well organized. It's open for anyone to attend and offers a far better educational opportunity than the public school that meets only three days a month.

At the school they put me to work teaching English, but mostly entertaining. I spent the night on a classroom floor and visited with the teachers who live at the school. It was a brief glimpse into another world: a world of people who are married, have children, but live and work far from them. They spoke English well, which allowed me to ask deeper questions about their lives, dreams, ideas and hopes. I discovered people with humble lives, simple desires and large hearts.

After a peek at the gompa and Buddhist monastery, I trekked onward to Pishue, the meeting place for my pony man. In addition, one of the nuns I had met on the bus from Manali was from there and had given me the address of her father's house. I've never found women with shaved heads attractive, but I must admit the nuns of Ladakh are beautiful in shaved heads. To her great surprise, I found Lobsang again, and we both laughed in our reunion.

I thought about why I was so attracted to her for some time. Part of it was a desiring of what one can't have; very human. But it was more than that; it was her gentleness, her giving and expecting nothing in return that made her so real and beautiful. I asked her once, "Don't you ever find yourself attracted to a man?" She said, "No, and if I did, I would just think of him as my brother." A very mature response for someone 21 years old, but then again, she'd left home to become a nun at 11 years of age. This is almost unthinkable in the west, but this was the only real chance of an education for women in a remote village. So the big brother I became, and she watched over me during my brief stay.

After reconnecting with my pony man, it was revealed to me that there were no ponies. That was a slight problem. I think he was planning on carrying my bag and had hoped I would just let go of having a pony man. So after a meeting of the minds, three hours later, I was in the company of a new pony man, who spoke only three words of English, and had two ponies.

Armed with only a bad map, off I went with my new pony man/cook/guide into the Zanskar wilderness. At the first night's campsite I discovered that the bag of veggies I saw the first pony man carrying wasn't along. It hadn't made the transfer. This meant for the next ten days I would be eating rice, dal (beans), and japoties (a kind of handmade pita bread) for breakfast, lunch and dinner. An ugly prospect. I knew I would live, if for no other reason than the pony man would see to it so there was someone to pay him at the end. I might start my own weight loss program and have it be this (rice, beans, bread), because I must have lost seven pounds that week (equal to one more notch on the belt).

Also that first night I had the good fortune of meeting Dorrine and Jan from Holland. It turned out that Jan was a travel writer from Holland, writing a guide on this particular trek. He had been here before, and was double-checking things. On top of that, he was a photographer and ecologist; we had much in common. Dorrine trekked at my pace, so the three of us just kind of melted together for the rest of the trip. For me it was such a gift to be with them. They were able to explain things along the way, and they saved me a couple of times from rice, dal and japoties. (I ended up feeding it more to the ponies than eating it.)

The trek in itself was amazing: the stark beauty of the barren, high mountains (that were tree-covered 150 years ago), contrasted occasionally by green patches in the valleys as the farmers eked out some barley. With the Indian/Pakistan scares the trek was deserted. There were days we saw no one. Other days we saw villagers who were probably wondering where everyone was, fearful of no tourist income for this year.

Climbing high mountain passes gave me open horizons, empty of everything except nature. In my trekking I saw similarities to my personal journey. Climbing ever upward toward the pass, with scenes of beauty around me, the pull and curiosity as to what the next valley looked like begged me onward. I would reach the top, with limitless views and open horizons. My soul seemed to expand, confined by nothing but my own imagination. Then the time would come to begin the journey down, down, down, with more splendid views. Before long, the next mountain pass whispered in the winds, "Come see what I have to share." The journey upward would once again begin.

And so is the cycle of life, with its ups and downs and all the scenes along the way. One scene is not better or worse than another. They are all part of the same journey, and to be cherished.

I rediscovered the hidden part in me that loves climbing high into the mountains. It is something that can only be experienced. Thus when the climb is completed, it floats away into the secret places in my heart, waiting to be rediscovered again and again. It is the common, unspoken bond that all people who love the mountains have. It's a deep love that lies beyond words and lives in the moment of the experience.

Eleven days later I arrived at the end of my trek, a little thinner and much dirtier than I began. But something happened to me inside on this particular journey. I had another shift within of calmness and inner peace.

It is hard to explain. I think there must be something magical that happens when one gets to explore a place like Zanskar and Ladakh. There, time has its own meaning.

It was a place snowed in, cut off, and isolated seven to eight months of the year. The smiles of the local people were timeless; they seemed to communicate what's really important in life. And if one was willing, this wisdom could get imprinted onto one's own soul. It was a special journey.

Arriving in Lamayaru, I stayed in a local guesthouse belonging to people I had met before. They were all excited to share with me a new DVD movie they had acquired of the WWF (World Wrestling Federation), or professional wrestling. Back into this crazy world I leaped, and soon found myself longing for the roadless valleys of Zanskar! It took me a few minutes to realize that they didn't know the WWF was acting; they thought it was completely real. This left me wondering how many people in the world are left thinking this was real. It should be no surprise that if this is the understanding others have of what it's like in the U.S., we have a big image problem. I slipped off to bed leaving them with Hulk Hogan and the rest of the gang.

It was good to get back to Leh. For two weeks I'd dreamed about the vegetable sizzler dish at the Pumpernickel German Bakery. I'd had it so many times when I was in Leh that the manager told me he was going to change the item's menu-name next year to *The Dean Sizzler*. People were coming into the restaurant asking for it by that name!

Within a couple of days I was getting bored in Leh, and decided it was time to move on. It was at this point that I went in search of the truth behind what's happening between Pakistan and India. I went to Kashmir, the forbidden travel destination according to the guidebooks; off limits to everyone who reads the news but never goes there. My journey took me through Kargil and on to Srinagar. Instead of taking a local bus, I opted for a shared taxi. Traveling with me were the manager of my guesthouse and Justine, a fellow traveler from Australia, on her way to meet a friend.

The first leg of our journey was uneventful. After a brief stay in Kargil, we were met with a closed road at 12:30 AM. Up ahead there was shooting and shelling going on between Pakistan and India that filled the valley/gorge with large booms and bangs. At first I thought we would probably turn the taxi around and head back to Kargil, but no. We stayed put with all the other taxis and trucks that clogged the road. We waited for the next five hours in the dark as the echoes of shells filled the air.

Eventually, tired and unable to sleep in the cramped jeep, I got out. I used my rain poncho for a ground cloth and sleeping bag for a blanket and spread them out on the ground. Justine joined me for a brief sleep, and I must confess it was nice to have her company. We were awakened at 5 AM by the beeping of the jeep horn in our ears. We dashed for the jeep with our sleeping things in our hands, and took off down the road like a bat out of hell. I couldn't tell if the driver usually drove this way or if this was an effort not to become someone's target. Either way, we made it to Srinagar, having passed many large military guns and fortifications along the way. I bid my riding companions farewell and went to find a bed for some much-needed rest.

Kashmir is called the "Garden of the Himalayans." It is understandable why. It's a scenic and beautiful place filled with every kind of greenery imaginable, all surrounded by majestic mountains. Once a summer haven for moguls (kings), it's now a deserted heaven waiting for peace. In Srinagar I lived like a king for a couple of days. I stayed on a houseboat whose owners fed me wonderful food.

One morning I hired a shikara, similar to a Venetian boat with a canopy, to row me around the lake like royalty all afternoon. In it I slept and rested as it glided across the water. I was treated very well; they were happy to see a western face. I stumbled onto a local man named Gulam, who was to become my guide for a couple of days. Kashmiris have a well-deserved reputation for overcharging tourists, so constantly bargaining for everything was the norm. Galum took care of all of that for me, and made sure I paid only local prices. It was a nice help and allowed me to relax a little.

Galum showed me around the city. We hopped onto local buses, auto-rickshaws, and into the back of horse-drawn carts. We explored Mosques, and even the so-called "Tomb of Jesus." One morning we took a local bus to a countryside lake. After a brief walk through some of the nearby villages, we went back to the lakeside that was packed with Sunday pic-nickers. Soon I found myself surrounded by young boys asking for my photo and my signature. I asked Galum to explain to them that I wasn't famous, but that didn't seem to slow them down.

My last night in Srinagar I moved to Galum's guest-houseboat. It was moored on the river rather than on Dal Lake. When it came time to eat dinner, Galum started mentioning that his brother was mentally ill. I didn't quite understand what he was talking about and let it pass by. At dinner I joined the family in the kitchen, which was where I found his 25-year-old brother sitting on a countertop. He looked perfectly normal to me as I had a brief conversation with him. A few minutes passed as I sat on the floor eating before I noticed the legs of the brother were chained to a post. It put me into a moment of shock and fear. "What was this?" my mind shouted. I couldn't comprehend, and my mind was racing to try to under-stand. Was this man so dangerous that I might be in danger? He looked so normal sitting there.

These were the types of thoughts that floated through my mind as I tried to carry on a normal conversation with Galum. I was afraid to look, because when I did, it was painful to see. I never asked Galum about his brother; I didn't know what to ask. All I can remember Galum saying was that he was mentally ill. Then I wondered about what happens to the mentally ill in poor countries; do they get locked up and hidden away? It's a question that I only half-heartedly wanted to know the answer to.

The next morning I once again hopped on a bus to my next destination, Katra. Katra is home to one of the most sacred Hindu pilgrimage sites in all of India: Vaishno Devi (the three mother-goddesses of Hinduism). Arriving at 6 PM, I show-ered and ate. By 9 PM I was headed up the mountainside to begin my own pilgrimage. With little information available to me, I figured the whole trip would take about four hours, which would put me back into my hotel bed by 1 AM.

The path upward was amazing, filled with Hindi pilgrims from all over India singing songs that expressed their love and devotion, such as, "Mother, I hear you calling, and I can't resist your call." I was quickly adopted by a group of young men who refused to let me buy anything for myself the entire trip. As the night wore on it began to become clear that I had done a miscalculation in my head about the time frame. It was 2 AM by the time we finally reached our destination. Whoops, that was five hours just getting there.

My walking mates guided me through all the proper rituals: the sacred shower to prepare for the meeting, bowing at the right times, wearing no leather. They also taught me the rally call, "Jai Mata Di," ("Victory to Mother Goddess"). When I would shout this out, it would always bring big smiles and a responding "Jai Mata Di!" We walked together in single file, working our way closer to the deities.

Eventually we came to a place that was much smaller than I had imagined, given the volume of people and all the excitement from the long walk. I had imagined a huge cave, and thought where I was might be a preliminary setting as people walked slowly by. But as I came to the spot, they stopped the entire procession. With complete gentleness and humility, they waved to me to come closer.

The Hindu Holy Man explained to me, with pure kindness in his eyes, who each deity was and what they meant to the Hindu people. I was deeply moved by the presence before me, and the respect they offered to me. Most pilgrims are allowed only a brief walk by, and here I was given a full audience. Smiling a grand smile, I repeated "dun ya bat" (thank you) several times and bowed to offer my own respect to this holy place and to those present.

According to legend, one must visit another site for the pilgrimage to be complete, which is located two kilometers up from there. So, off we went to finish this pilgrimage. We made our offerings and finally began the long trip down. By this time it was getting light again, and my body, after an all day bus ride and walking all night long, was beginning to wear out. At 10 AM, some 26 kilometers (15 miles) later, I dragged myself back into Katra to have a two-hour nap before catching my next bus to Jaumu. There I boarded my train to Amritsar and the Sikh's Golden Temple.

Way up north photographs   [72], page 127   [73], page 128   [74], page 129   [75], page 129
     [76], page 130   [77], page 131   [78], page 132

Entry Thirty-three: India - hail and farewell!

In a half-daze, I boarded the train with some people that I had met from Bombay. I was more than willing to just follow them to Amritsar. After another night train ride, we arrived early the next morning. We found a hotel close to the railway station and crashed for a couple of hours before heading out to the temple.

I have met all types of wonderful people in India, but the Sikhs are some of my favorite. As a community they are consistently kind, gentle and humble. They also have a reputation for having great courage and they make up 90% of the Indian army. I learned over time to look for them (they always had a beard and a turban hat) when I needed help or directions. Several times they approached me and would sincerely inquire if I needed any help. Their presence scared the hawkers away from me. They are India's guardian angels. It was these qualities that endeared them to me, fueling the desire to experience their holy place: The Golden Temple.

Briefly, the Golden Temple is a gold-plated building that sits in the middle of a square, man-made lake. More temple buildings also surround the lake. Everything is made of white marble, and is very clean. It's a peaceful place filled with worshipers of all ages. It was quite refreshing to step through the gates and into the sanctuary of this ancient place. After a brief stay we headed back to the hotel.

Two of my companions invited me to join them in going to the Pakistan-India border crossing to observe the nightly ceremony when both sides lower their national flags. When I arrived at the border I found a stadium-like atmosphere. On each side of the main gate was stadium-seating filled with onlookers. On the Pakistani side, the stadium was divided with men on one side, and women on the other. The Indian stadium, much larger in size, was a mass of humanity. I planted myself in the middle of this mass and witnessed what appeared to be a football game, then a changing of the guard. People were chanting, yelling and screaming slogans on both sides of the gate. The only thing that was missing was the yell: "We're Number 1!" Grown men made silly gestures like school children taunting each other into a fight. Personally, I think both sides have too many people bored with life who think a fight would liven things up a little. Unfortunately they happen to have nukes in their back pockets and seem unaware of the potential consequences, being lost in their emotions. We can only hope common sense will prevail, and peace will come.

Afterwards we hurried back to the train station. They boarded and left me alone to spend the night in Amritsar. I decided to wander back to the Golden Temple to get some night shots of the temple lit up against the nighttime sky. Arriving at the temple, I checked my daypack into the cloakroom and walked into the center area to see the beautifully illuminated Golden Temple reflected on the black lake.

I met a young Sikh from Delhi named Jimmy. He fit the image of a Sikh—big, bearded and kind. Jimmy convinced me to join him in taking a bath in the holy waters of the lake. After some searching, we purchased a pair of bathing shorts, changed, and went lakeside to the bathing location. I waded into the water, walking down the marble steps that slowly disappeared into the blackness. Surrounded by bathers on all sides, Jimmy was directly behind me, slowly wading in.

It was a beautiful sight, wading into the water with the golden reflection filling the surface of the lake. The water is supposed to be able to cleanse your soul. It was very conceivable in this golden water. As I was enjoying the quiet moment, I heard a man shrieking. It was Jimmy; he was afraid of the large fish (carp) that swam around his legs as he bathed. Suddenly he went running out of the water, unable to control his fear. I asked, "What happened to the fearless Sikhs of legend and lore?" I chuckled, asking him if he was afraid of being gummed to death! He just laughed, and said that *most* Sikhs were brave, not all!

We dried off and went to the kitchen where we plopped down on the floor and they fed us. Generally I get a spoon, but not here. It was time to eat with my fingers. So, mopping up rice and dal as best as I could, I filled up and relished the moment. It finally came time to go, so we went to the cloakroom to get our things, only to be greeted by a locked window. They had just closed, the room was dark, and it wouldn't open again until three the next morning.

I was stuck. My shoes were in my bag, along with my other personal items, so I was going nowhere. We went back into the temple, knowing I would be able to catch my 6 AM train. But once again this meant getting no sleep for the third night in a row.

We found an open space lakeside on the marble bank, plopped down and tried to rest. I thought to myself, "This is a pretty nice place to be stuck." The cool marble felt good against my warm skin, and I used my water bottle as a pillow. I spent the next four hours watching the temple, staring at the stars in the nighttime sky and floating in and out of sleep. I bathed, ate, and slept at the temple. They told me that should make me fairly pure for some time. (I'll take whatever help I can get!)

Eventually 3 AM arrived. I grabbed my bag and went back to my hotel. I took another shower, packed up, and headed to the train station to catch my early morning train to Delhi. I was knackered, as they say in Britain, but still kicking and now pure!

Waiting in Delhi was Sunita, a former travel companion in Ladakh. She had invited me to stay with her family while passing through that part of India. I instantly felt at home there; it was like visiting my family. In the home were Sunita's parents, and her brother, his wife and their three children. I was made to feel a part of the family, as the young twins called me uncle. It was good to be in such a loving environment, with the fun and laughter of small children.

Delhi was a "to-do list stop" for me. I finished up my Christmas shopping (for 2002), got my teeth cleaned at the dentist's office, cleaned myself up, sewed up torn clothes, purchased my airline ticket for Turkey, and most notably, cut my hair short. It was fun to have long hair and, its purpose being served, it was time for it to come off! It felt sssssssooooo good! Short is easy, cheap and best!

After finishing up my "to do" list, (by the way, I haven't missed having a "to-do" list one bit!) I hopped onto a train for Agra, home of the Taj Mahal. Even with all the touristy hype, this place is amazing. It is as close to perfection as you can get in regards to creating a physical structure. A fitting tribute to the depth of love the Mogul had for his wife, and in some way, what all men feel for their partners in life. It was blazing hot when I was there, but even that couldn't detract from the awe of this place.

Later that evening I sneaked onto the train with no ticket, and jumped off at Mathura. For a brief and somewhat rushed period, I explored the birthplace of Krishna, and then jumped back onto the train again the next morning. This time I wasn't so lucky; I stepped right into the arms of the conductor who immediately asked for my ticket. I said I wanted to buy a ticket, but he just kept asking for it, apparently not understanding what I was saying. This went on for a few moments, until I finally reached in and gave him the only ticket I had, my Delhi to Bombay ticket. He looked at it for a minute and finally asked me for 200 rupees ($4), the fee for my ticket and fine for boarding without it. I can handle that.

My return to Delhi was brief, just long enough to say good-bye, mail some boxes, and grab my backpack. Once again I was on a night train, this time heading for Bombay. Arriving in Bombay amidst constant rain, I decided to continue straight on to Pune. I have known many people who have passed through Pune, liked all of them, and was curious about what was there. In Pune I found a place to relax, and a chance to meditate as much as I wanted. It was a good way to finish up an amazing journey through India. Hours of silent meditation allowed me to reflect upon my experiences and keep them from disappearing into one, large, blurry haze.

India is a place of extremes: great wealth and great poverty; great inner peace and external chaos, with high-pitched emotions calling for war; people smashed together in large cities and the empty landscapes of Ladakh. It is a place where it is impossible not to be changed in a deep and profound way by what is experienced. One feels smothered: smothered by the neediness of the poor; smothered by the kindness of ordinary people; smothered by the different perspective of personal space and the curiosity of the people; smothered by the pollution and by the beauty of the land and the eyes of the people. In all of it I was exposed to the many faces of humanity, and in this I found a deeper understanding of myself. I'm not different, but a part of it all. And in some simple way, I found great peace in that.

Back in Bombay I stayed with the Amin family, whom I met on a pilgrimage in Jammu. Like the long lost cousin, we reunited for a brief moment. They took such good care of me. They whisked me around Bombay for the nickel tour and then put me on the plane.

India is now, and will forever be, alive in me. And hopefully, I was able to share with it the best part of myself.

India: Hail and farewell photograph   [79], page 132

Entry Thirty-four: Whoa! Life is different

Stepping off the plane in Dubai, the capital of the United Arab Emirates (UAE), was like walking through a time machine back into the first world, and all the shock that comes with that. For the last eight months I had been traveling in the third world, and what that brings. Thankfully Chris Peach, a friend I'd met in Nepal, was there to meet me at the airport.

I felt like a wide-eyed child in the UAE. Everything was new, shiny, and overwhelming. Whoa! The first couple of days, I felt like I couldn't get enough to eat. I craved foods like raw veggies and salads. Like someone on a diet who was not able to eat his favorite foods but endlessly was sneaking a bite, I ate and ate. Finally, after a couple of days that ended, and I was back to veggies and rice, with chicken (KFC style).

This country was such a stark contrast to where I had been: India's poverty and kindness, versus the UAE's wealth and emotional distance. I've come to my own conclusion that most wealthy people are boring, consumed by a never-ending hunger to hoard more stuff. Of course there are exceptions to this, but the trend is there.

Being with Chris and his wife Julie was like visiting old college mates. They were loads of fun and laughter, as we spent time "taking the piss" out of each other. It seemed that they were just what the doctor ordered as I rested up for my next leg of the journey, and as I waited for the mystery package from home.

It was so hot there. I wore my sunglasses not only for brightness, but also because the wind hurt my eyes. If I stepped outside for longer than 15 minutes ... stick a fork in me: I was well done! I took a drive one day and all I saw was sand, rocks, a beach, and of course sizzling heat: 110+ F or 40-45 C! I wondered how the people ever ate before ships and airplanes brought everything in! Another bummer was taking photos. The moment I stepped out of the air conditioning, my camera lens would fog up. All I could see through the viewfinder was gray.

I did enjoy meeting the local workers in the shops. They were from every place imaginable, and were quite nice. Julie and Chris watched over me so well!

Eventually I gave up waiting for my package, and assumed that it was now a part of someone's collection of objects that will never be seen again by the rightful owner.

So I prepared to move on to Turkey.

Whoa! Life is different photograph   [80], page 132

Entry Thirty-five: Merhaba ("hello" in Turkish)

The red, full moon hung over the horizon of Istanbul as I sat on the rooftop of my hostel drinking a beer. I was taking a moment to allow the beauty of such a sight to sink in and land in a quiet place. Truthfully, I was caught off-guard by Istanbul. How had a beautiful, ancient and significant place escaped me for so long? But, rather than go off on that tangent, I'll share my experience.

Stepping off the plane into the much cooler air of Turkey made me sigh in relief. The next day I went straight away to obtain a visa for Syria. Everyone was telling me about all the problems I would encounter, but of course no one really knew; they'd only heard stories. It turned out to be very easy and simple. And within a day I had my visa in hand. In the meantime, I explored Istanbul by foot and ferry.

Sitting between the Marmara and the Black Sea, Istanbul is a treasure chest of endless green landscapes and red roof-tops punctuated by the minarets of the mosques. Cutting through the heart of it all is the Bosphorus Channel, the dividing line between Asia and Europe. There they joke about how people work in Europe and sleep in Asia each night.

On one excursion, I entered a hotel and sneaked up to the top floor to soak up the free view. I had no idea Istanbul was so big (15 million people). It became understandable why, over such a long period of time, this city had been the seat of empires.

One place in particular that moved me was the Aya Sofya, designed to be the finest house of worship in the world in 532 AD. Wow, for almost one thousand years this was the largest church in the Christian world! After the conquest of Istanbul by Mehmed in 1453, it was turned into a mosque. In the 1930s, it was wisely turned into a museum by the famous president of Turkey, Ataturk, whom they claim as the father of modern Turkey. That's the boring part.

Once inside I stood in awe at the sheer size of this place. Gigantic in size, I struggled to find a place to take a photo that could convey its grandeur. The marble floor and steps had the shine, wear and dips that could only come from hundreds of years of use. As I walked around the interior, I kept having this deep sense that I had been here before, a long, long time ago. The walls and the floor felt painfully familiar to my touch. The light shining through the windows from high above seemed to pierce through time into the distant past. The mosaics on the walls wanted to speak, but stayed silent, keeping the secrets of the past. I lay on the floor and looked up to the ceiling. I would have lain there for hours had they not kicked me out at closing time. I said my prayers and left.

I enjoy large cities, but never enough to stay for long periods of time. It is on the road where you meet the interesting people, and the adventures generally occur. For a few days I was in Europe before heading back to Asia again. Once there I turned south, down the coast of Turkey.

Transportation in Turkey is easy in that there are frequent buses and ferries everywhere. I headed out with the ancient city of Troy as my destination. With the help of local people who almost took me by the hand to make sure I found the right bus, I arrived in Canakkale.

The next morning found me walking through the ancient ruins of Troy: the location of the war in which the famous Trojan horse was used to defeat the city. I came to appreciate history in a deeper way as the guide explained what we know of Troy and the role it played throughout time. He told how, with the writings of Homer, myth and fact blended into a great story of love and conquest. Without a guide I would have been totally lost for sure, my knowledge of history being a tad-bit weak. But with my imagination and his information, I was swept back in time for a brief moment, with a view of a bay filled with ships stopped over in Troy, and streets filled with merchants and traders from abroad. It was pretty cool.

Later that day I blended as best I could into the droves of Aussies and Kiwis making their pilgrimage to the battlefields of Gallipoli. This place is where thousands lost their lives in a botched attempt to invade the Ottoman Empire during WWI. Our Turkish guide told us stories of great courage and compassion. He told of the unbelievable respect the two sides have for each other. This is the place where the Aussies and the Kiwis became nations. It was a defined period in time where two nations were born out of a nasty experience.

Out of my love and respect for these three countries, I went there to learn and understand more. Today the entire area is a memorial for all sides involved. The dead from both sides lay side by side, honored together by the Turkish people. This says a great deal about the Turks. In the end, many heroes and legends were created in this 270-day battle. But I couldn't shake the thought that there must be a better way than war to create heroes.

Merhaba: "Hello" in Turkish photographs   [81], page 133   [82], page 134   [83], page 134

Entry Thirty-six: Big jumps

Heading further down the coast, I landed in Selcuk. Here I strolled through the ruins of Ephesus. Like salmon swimming in a crowded stream, the tourists (me included) flooded the sight with busloads of camera-toting westerners.

Having said this, Ephesus is still very impressive. It is home to one of the best-preserved ancient Roman cities on the eastern Mediterranean. It was here that St. John preached, most likely in the very theater where I sat. It brought the Bible to life. Also while in Selcuk, I paid homage at the location where the Virgin Mary spent the last years of her life, now a small and beautiful chapel in the woods.

After a brief stay and a mud bath in Koycegiz, I headed for Fethiye, a resort town on the Mediterranean coast. At this point I was travelling with some Kiwis and a token Aussie. I had fallen into a pattern of following their agenda because I enjoyed their company. They were on holiday, doing holiday things, which generally was a bit more "spendy." I noticed myself getting restless. I knew that soon I would have to find something more ordinary and more realistic as to what it means to live and be Turkish.

But before leaving the well-beaten tourist path, I decided to do a paragliding jump. This consisted basically of running off a cliff with a parachute tied to your back. So, one morning a truckload of us rode up to the top of a nearby mountain. One by one, with a pilot strapped to us, we ran into the wind and off the cliff. The wind lifted us off the ground in less than five steps, and suddenly my feet were left dangling above the ground far below. The 40-minute trip was an unforgettable ride, with views of blue Mediterranean lagoons and bays on one side, and the rolling hills and mountains of inland Turkey on the other. With an "eehhhaaa" we landed safely on the beach. I did have a few scary moments as my mind imagined what a fall to the ground or into the water would be like (mostly what the landing would be like, not the falling part), but I somehow decided it was wasted thought, and just enjoyed the ride!

One last tourist stop, but not so touristy: I made a trip to see Cappadocia, a land with amazing rock formations and underground cities built by early Christians for safety. I half-expected to see Fred Flintstone running around. Many houses and buildings looked like they popped right out of the cartoon. Generally, I was impressed by the measures those

Christians took in order to survive and practice their faith. Eventually the authorities got smart and gave a huge tax break if you were Muslim, which was very effective. And what that didn't handle, the large ethnic exchange after WWI with Greece did handle, leaving ghost towns and forgotten underground cities.

The place is loaded with sites, and after three days I was rock-and-caved-out. So I rented a moped and went to explore villages where no one speaks English and no tourists can be found. At the end of that day I was so happy. There is something special about a day when, at the end of it, I can go to bed knowing I did what I love to do!

From here, it was east, east, east and less, less tourists.

Big jumps photograph   [84], page 135   [85], page 135

Entry Thirty-seven: Some deep thoughts, 16 months into the journey

For the better part of my life, I have lived with a feeling or sense that someday I will reach my potential. This would leave me in a state of feeling that I hadn't accomplished what I'm capable of achieving.

It's important not to collapse this with the simple truth that we are constantly growing and changing with time, or with the practice of setting a high goal and finding ways to fulfill that objective. What I'm talking about is the deep sense of peace and passion that wells up from inside when one does exactly that which is one's purest and deepest desire. Often we get caught up in the "doing-ness" and business of life so we forget to look inside and examine what motivates us to take (or not take) actions.

This is not checking out from life in some dreamy nonsense, but rather bringing to it every part of oneself each and every moment. Instead of escaping through drugs, television, work, sports, travel, dramas and the like, one becomes aware of how precious every moment in life is. How one can do this is part of what we are here to discover. It is not something one can read about and then go do. Instead, it is a blend of experience and the desire to live life to the fullest.

You do not need to seek the approval of others to say that you are on the right track. It will be clear in the way it shows up in those around you. It doesn't mean you ignore the counsel of trusted friends, or the information that arises to help make decisions. It's just that the final decision is yours and yours alone. It will go with you to bed at night and rise with you in the morning. When made from as pure a place in your heart as possible, you then trust the outcome as part of what you are to learn here.

It doesn't mean that when one finds this place, only good things are going to happen. Many times it's the opposite. What this does mean is that one can never live a numbed-out life of existence, going through the motions, hoping to make it from point A to point B. With this realization comes the great joys and great pains of life.

This is a part of what I am discovering and experiencing on this journey. That place in me that once felt I "wasn't quite there yet" has faded away and has been replaced with a deep sense of awe and joy. I still feel the pain, and have the sufferings that are inescapable, but they are not given special attention and blown out of proportion.

A colleague of mine from my S-TESL (School of Teaching English as a Second Language) class in Seattle emailed me a question at the beginning of my trip. Alan asked me if it was necessary to take such a long journey to acquire the truth. I responded at the time that I couldn't answer the question, because at that point it was impossible for me to know. I've come to my own answer for his question: Yes, for me, the journey was and is necessary.

For me there is no substitute for experience. I could read about the world, watch endless hours of the National Geographic Channel or the Discovery Channel and never have gained the wisdom that comes from looking people in their eyes and exchanging smiles. I want to *know* this world, not only in the sense of facts, but also a knowing that I am a part of it. I want to taste it, smell it, touch it, and feel it. I want to laugh and cry with my fellow brothers and sisters, together as one.

And in some way I want to do what I can to contribute to this small blue dot in space that we all share. In that I feel like a one-man, unofficial, world ambassador for the U.S. I bring a human face to the images people see on television, and the reality that we, in the States, aren't all endless piles of money or hoping to go to war with anyone we want. I do my best to answer questions and have my actions express that we are more alike than different. I listen to the stories, hopes and dreams of people and in turn, share with them the same. If I can somehow bridge these two places, in some small way, then I will have accomplished something on a grand scale. For me, it is a challenge worthy of my precious and short stint here.

Entry Thirty-eight: Where's John Wayne when you need him?

Dogubayzit, which I pronounce "Dogbiscuit," sits at the base of the massive Mt. Ararat. Situated on the Iranian border in eastern Turkey, Mt. Ararat is an impressive mountain that shoots up into the sky some 5,190 meters (16,500 feet). Ararat is famous for being the supposed resting-place for Noah's Ark, and all the things of legend. It sounded adventurous so I decided to make an ascent of the mountain.

I asked around the town and discovered all the guides wanted anywhere from $150 to $500 dollars to make the climb. That's a ridiculous amount of money for three days of climbing. After some searching around, I found a young couple from the Czech Republic and a young Israeli who also wanted to climb without paying so much money. We found a local guide who was willing to drop us off and pick us up at the trailhead, allowing us to climb alone. We would have to pay some money to pad the pockets of the checkpoints and climb without a permit. That sounded *really* adventurous, so off we went and up the mountain we climbed.

Mt. Ararat is a deceptive mountain. It looked close as it sat there taunting me to climb. There are no trees, only rocks with patches of occasional green grass where sheep come to graze. On the top sit white glaciers that are often shrouded by clouds.

We got a late start the first day, not leaving until 2:30 PM. With all of our gear on our backs and one bad map, up we headed for the first camp. My hiking companions walked much faster, leaving me pretty much to walk alone. I didn't mind though; I love walking in nature and in solitude.

By the time I finally caught up with them they had already set up camp and were preparing to eat—good timing on my part. In addition, it was fast getting dark and we would soon be bedding down for the night. The night was not so restful; once again my stomach was rebelling. But that was nothing compared to our morning.

At about 5:30 AM, the zipper of our tent slowly went up and a shotgun barrel came poking in. "Uh oh," I thought. "It's the army coming to get us for climbing without a permit." It wasn't. Instead, as the zipper went further up it revealed a young man with a blue silk handkerchief across his face like some character in a western movie. As he was holding an ancient twelve-gauge single-barreled shotgun pointed right at us, we weren't going anywhere fast. The other tent with the Czech couple also had a visitor holding a pistol, demanding the same thing: money, money, and money!

As I sat in my underwear inside my sleeping bag, I thought, "Hmm, this is interesting." Our bandit gave us the courtesy of breaking his gun barrel to show us it was loaded and ready. Shay, my tent mate, and I were pretty much left alone after I lightened my load and gave him the $150 I had on me. The Czech couple was having more problems. They had no money with them and the bandits thought they were hiding it. They emptied out their backpacks and tore things apart looking for money. In a moment of frustration the bandits took the pistol, pointed it at their heads and then pointed it into the air firing a shot to try and scare them into giving them money.

I was more concerned about my camera and gear than my money; money is easier to replace. After realizing they had all of our money, they started yelling for a cell phone: "Phone, phone, phone!" We had no phone. Eventually they fled, telling us in some kind of strange language not to leave the tent for one hour. I wanted to go after them, but my tent mate was shaken up and asked me to stay. I'm not sure what I was going to do anyway; throw rocks at them, maybe?

After a cup of tea we decided to march upward and stay closer together. Our ride was not due for two days and we had no way of contacting him. In addition, with no permit we weren't even supposed to be there, so going to the police was not a real option. As we climbed higher, we were constantly scanning the horizon looking for the next gang to come riding up. After climbing all morning we finally reached high camp, the jumping-off point for the summit.

Physically and emotionally exhausted from the morning, we lay in our tents trying to get some rest. Suddenly in the wind we heard some voices. Our tents were surrounded by a rock wall built by past climbers for protection from the wind, so the tents were hidden from view. Creeping out of our tents, we grabbed our ice axes and peeked over the top of the wall to see what was out there. We saw no one, but now our minds were working and we came up with a battle plan in case we had a second encounter. (But jeesh, rocks and ice axes against guns are not good odds!)

Thankfully the Czechs spotted a climbing party down below us. We knew that now we could rest because the chances of something else happening went down dramatically. Waking up at 5 AM (on our own this time), we poked our heads out of the tent to discover snow pellets and clouds: not a good sign. I had winter gear but my climbing mates didn't. After waiting for three hours, we made the disappointing decision to abandon the climb. It just seemed like we weren't supposed to climb that mountain; all manner of events were occurring to make sure we didn't.

Now ahead of us was the climb down and, in our minds, into bandit territory. We cautiously approached the climbing parties below, feeling unsure about whom we could trust. With a little careful talking, we were able to call our driver and change our meeting time to earlier in the day. Sensing the worst was over, we decided to maintain height to our advantage and follow the ridge down, giving us the view.

We breathed a sigh of relief to see our driver walking up the trail to meet us. Once in the car, we explained to the driver what had happened to us. We went to the village to sort out what to do from there. He asked what they looked like. "Well," I said, "they had dark skin, black hair and brown eyes." ("That eliminates about five percent of Turkey," I thought.)

As we explained our story, one of the older women listening, who apparently lives much of her time high on the mountain, asked, "Why didn't you fight them? They were two; you were four." I responded by saying, "It was a little rough given I was in my underwear, trapped in my tent looking down the barrel of a twelve-gauge shotgun. I didn't even have a rock to throw!" She just smiled with her few teeth and lit up a cigarette. Eventually she said, "Next time you come with me and we will have a smoke up on the mountain." Knowing there would not be a next time, I just said, "OK," as we walked out the door.

Soon I was saying goodbye again to my travel companions as our experience was transforming into my latest travel adventure. What did I learn from all this? A guide up Mt. Ararat isn't necessary; the route is clear enough and direct. But an armed bodyguard is a good idea!

Where's John Wayne when you need him? photograph   [86], page 136

Entry Thirty-nine: The end of Turkey

As I worked my way back through western Turkey, I encountered some friends I had made in Nepal. There they were, Arnoe and Kathy, heading west after crossing through Iran.

It was always a great and enjoyable surprise to meet up with those I'd met earlier, especially when they were people I liked. We traveled together for a few days across Lake Vangh in local buses. The buses were stopped every ten miles to check passports and look for Kurdish rebels. At one stop we stayed in a village with a local man and his family. We slept on the floor of his house, chatted with his wife and twelve children, glimpsing life for this Kurdish family. They were kind, humble and giving.

We continued west, and at some point I stayed on the bus as Arnoe and Kathy got off, alone again in my journey. I had a specific place I was aiming for now: Konya, home of Rumi and the whirling dervishes. After my all-night bus ride, I arrived in Konya at 4 AM.

In a sleepy haze, I got off the bus, grabbed my bags and started walking toward the city center. Eventually, after getting picked up by a drunken taxi driver and his college friend, I found a place to rest. Later that day I woke up, and rummaged through my bag to put on my hat. However, I discovered that I had left it on the bus. This time there was no chasing after it; only the pain of letting go. I was so bummed, and there was nothing to do but find a new hat.

While in Konya I was treated to a special demonstration of the dervishes that was more than enough to make up for the loss of my hat. Additionally, I couldn't resist and bought a Turkish rug. I had concluded that I want to live a simple life, with fewer things to clutter up. But I want the things I do have around to add beauty, in a simple and elegant way. So, one day I will have a space to live and in that space will lay a beautiful Turkish rug.

Turkey is a surprise in many ways, rich in history and overflowing with places to explore. The people are warm and friendly. It embodies the crossroads of east and west: Women dressed in headscarves walk along the streets next to women dressed in skin-tight, revealing clothing. Men carry Islam prayer beads and read the section in the paper with photos of naked women. Fast-moving sports cars pass horse-drawn carts coming from the fields onto the roadside. The country is so crazy about football (soccer) that the streets become ghost-like during a big match.

I'm not sure where Turkey is in all of this and I get the feeling they're not sure either, which made it an interesting place to explore. I continued my trip south to head for Syria.

The end of Turkey photographs   [87], page 137   [88], page 137   [89], page 138

Entry Forty: Moving back in time

Crossing the border into Syria turned out to be an uneventful moment. The western travelers were clumped together in the immigration building. The women dressed with scarves over their heads; we guys dressed more conservatively.

Not wanting to risk problems, we sat quietly, smiling at those who seemed interested in us. At one point I even pulled out my camera, normally a taboo in or around government buildings, and took some photos of a beautiful young Muslim girl. Entering into one of the "axis of evil" countries turned out to be dull.

Syria wasn't originally on my route. But since it was on the way to Jordan, rather then fly over, I crossed over it by land. Right from the start Syria felt different. Gone were the brands of the west. The western countries either boycott or have an embargo on Syria. Whatever the case, it meant signs of the west were missing; but in my case, not missed. There was no lack, however: "Coke-a-Cola" was made by a local company as were potato chips, so I wasn't going to starve. This lent itself to a unique experience because I really felt like I was in a foreign place.

My first destination was Aleppo, an ancient (a term which seems to get used all too often in the Middle East) trading center between Asia and Europe. For a couple of days I wandered through the souq (pronounced "suke"), the covered, narrow streets that have been the market for hundreds of years.

I strolled through the Christian quarter, a new concept for me. I tried to get some sense of what it meant to be a Christian in a predominantly Muslim state. It was Sunday and everything was closed; yet the rest of the city was a buzz of activity. I stepped into a Catholic Church and sat through a part of some kind of Boy Scout-looking ceremony. There I was at least able to observe some normal life. The women looked and dressed very western, and seemed to have a propensity for hair spray. I was asked not to sit with my legs crossed, to which I politely obliged. After about 20 minutes, I got bored and slipped out the back door.

The market was filled with everything imaginable, smells and sights that probably have changed little over the years. I saw carcasses of sheep hanging in front of the butcher shops dripping blood into pans, and rolls of beautiful material waiting to be sewn into some kind of ornate garment. There were bags of spices, coffee beans and teas that filled the air with special aromas. All types of gold jewelry filled some small windows. Women's brassieres dangled in doorways. It was a far cry from Wal-Mart and ever so much more interesting!

In the evening, on the rooftop of my hostel, I joined in some interesting conversations. My companions were a young Dutch girl on her way to the Palestinian territories to work on conflict issues with children, a young Norwegian woman studying human rights, a doctor from Iran, three Japanese who spoke little English, and a young German couple from Berlin. All of us (except the doctor) were sleeping on the roof sandwiched between honking horns from below, and the star-filled sky above.

In Syria I found a different kind of traveler: one that wasn't scared away by the propaganda and who was interested in experiencing the culture as well as looking at old stones. We seemed to form a kinship of common ground, and as we traveled across Syria and Jordan, we would frequently see each other and have small reunions. Our conversations were kept to the rooftop of our hostel; sensitive conversations in Syria draw the wrong kind of attention.

It was in these conversations that I was able to begin to flesh out in my own mind some small understanding of the distinctions of Arab, Islam, fundamentalism and its various forms. It had been for me like the view from our rooftop: all buildings were the same shade of light tan, a monolithic hue of various shapes and sizes. After absorbing as much information and beer as I could, I would slip into my rooftop nest and stare at the stars until fading off to sleep.

One morning I woke up and decided it was time to go. Telling my new friends that my gut told me it was time to move on, I left. Then while on the bus to my intended destination, I had a conversation with an Italian woman traveling with her mother. "Pretty cool," I thought, and decided to continue on with them for an additional three hours. This is one of the great joys of traveling solo; you get to change your mind instantly and be surprised by where you step off the bus.

On the last leg of that ride, I met Rene and Annamiek, a Dutch couple from Amsterdam. Traveling the same direction, they were to become my next companions. Rene's humor and Annamiek's spunk were welcomed company and added much spice to the journey. We stepped off the bus in Palmyra, home of some amazing Greek and Roman ruins. It was once a great city in the middle of nowhere. What makes it so special is the grand size of it all, some 50 hectares of land. But more importantly to me was the fact that nobody else was there. There was a small handful of us; that was it.

One evening I had the opportunity to go for a walk through the ruins under the star-filled sky with an American woman named Holly. As we walked through the pillars, she shared with me what she had learned earlier in the day from her tour guide. Looking up at the pillars with the nighttime sky as a backdrop was very moving. As we sat in the Roman theater looking up at the stars, it felt like a scene from a movie. A magical experience: a combination of timeless, ancient and present moments mixed together in the warm nighttime air. It was too bad that Holly was only on a one-week tour of the Middle East.

After getting my fill of photos, I left Palmyra to find what has been called the greatest castle in the world, Krak des Chevaliers. Arriving at my next bed on a rooftop, I discovered my friends from Aleppo. We made plans to share a minivan tour. The following morning we were on our way to see "The Krak," as the locals call it, when we pulled into a Bedouin campsite familiar to the driver for a tea stop.

The Bedouin people are reknowned for their friendliness and gracious hospitality. As our guide translated, we got to peek into the lives of these nomadic people. The mother, who had a beautiful smile containing a few golden teeth amongst the white, told us she had 15 children and she was 40 years old. "Whoa," I thought, "Same age as me with 15 children..." I asked her if she would be having any more. She just smiled and said, "Inshallah," which means "God willing."

After the usual various conversations, the showing of my photos, and the all-too-familiar chat about why I'm not married, we packed up and left. They invited me to stay for a few days, and for a brief moment I had daydreams of living a Bedouin life. Had I been alone, I might have accepted the invitation. I think they were cooking up plans to get me married off. Once again I escaped. But it might have made an interesting book!

Arriving at the Krak, we jumped out of the van, bending our heads backward to take in the enormous size of the castle sitting on top of a mountain. Built by the Crusaders, who seem to have spent a lot of time building castles, this place seemed to pop right out of the storybooks. Walking around the castle it wasn't hard to imagine the days when knights filled the mess hall, servants raced around taking care of things, and horses were in the stables waiting to be ridden off to the next battle. I kept thinking, "Wow, what a great place to be a kid." Well, the kid in me was happy!

That evening we landed in Damascus, capital of Syria. People have been living here since as long ago as 5,000 BC. It's hard for me to grasp that, being from a country that is only 225 years old. It has a long history, too long for me to relate in detail. Besides, there are plenty of history books for that.

I cherry-picked my spots in Damascus, going to the place where the disciples lowered St. Paul out of a window so he could flee from the Jews after he had preached in the synagogues, the Chapel of Ananias (an early Christian disciple), and the Umayyad Mosque. I spent an afternoon sleeping in the Umayyad Mosque, one of the three most holy mosques for Islam. Sitting in the mosque, I watched pilgrims who had come from abroad to fulfill their pilgrimage. It was moving to watch and experience such devotion. The inside of the mosque was as peaceful as a meadow in the mountains, and an easy place to commune with the divine. While I sat inside and watched the many people go through the ritual motions, I slipped off to sleep and took a nap where I was cloaked in a pool of devotion and love. I found some rest.

Walking through the narrow streets of the souq, I came across a bakery. They were baking bread, probably the same way they have for hundreds of years. An opening into a large clay oven revealed a bright red hue inside from the fire. With a long stick that had a flattened end like a paddle, they would move bread in and out of the oven. People were lined up to buy bread, exchanging smiles with me as I soaked up the scene.

One man reached into his bag and gave me one of the flat round loaves of bread from inside. Smiling at me he said, "Please take." I graciously accepted his offer, and he asked me where I was from. I told him the U.S. He then said, "Welcome, most welcome. Maybe you can go home and tell your people that the people of Syria are kind and not what media says."

Which is so true: the ordinary people of Syria are very kind and friendly. The governmental system is a different story, but the ordinary people are genuinely friendly. That's a quality that I can appreciate coming from the Midwest part of America. I never shied away from telling people that I was from the States. I figure it's as important for them as it is for me to know each other as we are, rather than what is portrayed in the media. I replied, "I promise to do so."

There is little gained by calling a country an "axis of evil." Actually, doing so does harm, and peace is pushed farther away. Period. The people I have encountered were mature enough to be able to differentiate between my government and me. And rather than attack, they used the opportunity to build a friend instead of create an enemy—which is more than I can say for the Falwells of our country. But that's another story.

I left Syria headed for Jordan, feeling like I understood a little more about the people and the country than when I came. That was enough for now. Catching the bus at first light, I headed for Amman, Jordan. I had an invitation from my Norwegian friends to join them for a night at the ambassador's home, *inshallah*.

Moving back in time photographs   [90], page 139   [91], page 139   [92], page 140
                                           [93], page 140   [94], page 140

Entry Forty-one: Indiana Jones, move over

The ride from Damascus to Amman, Jordan, is really a short trip, but one that thrust me back into the 21st century.

Gone were the streets with 50's classic cars serving as taxis, and back were the flashy-dressed Jordanians with cell phones glued to their ears. I followed my Norwegian friends to the ambassador's residence (actually as Hilde called her, "the ambassador-in-training") to sleep in a real bed for a night. After sleeping on rooftops and using semi-clean bathrooms for a while, a posh residence was a welcomed shock. We laughed about the luxury of each having our own private bathroom to use whenever we wanted. The ambassador-in-training was gone, but she had made arrangements for us to be picked up at the bus stop and brought to the house.

The place was so nice. It had white marble floors throughout the entire house, a patio to sit out on and have a cup of coffee, and a cable system with 1,000 channels! Later that night we reunited with the rest of our traveling friends and found an Irish pub, which you can find in almost every city in the world. I spent half the night dancing with the most beautiful Jordanian woman. Her dancing ability kept me in a trance with the way she moved her body. It was too bad she spoke no English, but her constant smile was enough communication for me!

An impromptu gathering after the bar found us discussing politics once again and playing a game called "I've Never." Finally at 5 AM, I decided I was getting too old for this stuff and collapsed into bed. The ambassador returned home the next afternoon, and we gave her a load of thanks for allowing us to stay there before saying goodbye. I never saw one tourist attraction while in Amman, which I didn't mind a bit. My main reason for coming to Jordan still lay ahead: Petra.

When I began my trip, I had never heard of Petra. I had seen it in an Indiana Jones movie, but didn't know it actually existed. Then somewhere along the way I saw a jacket cover for an airline ticket with a sketch of Petra. I said to myself, "I don't know where that is, but wherever it is, I'm going there." And thus Jordan was added to my itinerary.

That was ten months before, and suddenly there I was, standing at the entrance of Petra. Walking through the narrow canyon had an adventurous feeling to it as it winds around, first expanding and then getting narrow. Its depth is amazing and magical, because at certain points it gets so narrow you could probably jump from one side to the other. Twisting its way through the rock formations with chiseled-out tomb fronts and an irrigation channel carved into the side of the walls, the passageway leads you to an amazing tomb called "the treasury."

The place of the Jones filming, the very narrow, shadow-filled walkway leads you to the foot of this incredible and majestic tomb front that appears to be stamped into the side of the canyon wall. With its grand pillars, influenced by the Greek and Roman styles, this place is a storybook come to life. The lack of tourism and the sheer size of this place made it easy for me to become the explorer we all have in ourselves, out to discover a lost and forgotten civilization.

My companions and I had gone separate directions earlier in the day. Sitting alone in the silence I watched the occasional tourist wander by, awed in the wonderment of how anyone could carve such things. I concluded that for sure they had a different relationship to time, and an appreciation that, sometimes, beautiful creations take time. (And probably in this case, some slave labor.)

As the daylight was coming to an end, Andy the Australian wild man wandered my way, and we headed home together along with Kay, a South Dakota traveler who was taking the long road home. We were the last ones to leave the area, and with darkness closing in fast we opted for a donkey ride through the canyon. Racing our slow-moving donkeys, humming out loud the theme from the Indiana Jones movies, our laughing voices echoed through the corridors of rock before disappearing into the silent darkness.

I believe that in each of us lives the idea of, or spirit of, an Indiana Jones. This spirit is the part of us that loves to explore, to discover new things, new lands, and new people. It is in these discoveries we also discover a part of ourself. And since we are ever-changing, that process is never-ending. Some choose to honor it, others choose to ignore it, but nonetheless it is always in us, waiting for the chance to come forth, to blossom in the light of the newness of things patiently waiting.

Petra was special in that it called me to come explore. I trusted its call, and its promise held true: there was magic in Petra waiting to be experienced. After two days in Petra, our group headed for the desert to celebrate Rene's birthday: his wish to be with friends in the nighttime desert was to come true. So for two nights we wandered around the desert as part of a packaged tour. Designed for backpackers like us, the tour was cheap and fun.

Sleeping outside underneath the nighttime desert sky is unlike anything else. You have the biggest screen in front of you, offering incredible secrets and stories if you watch closely. With the familiar and unfamiliar once again offering a blanket overhead, I often awakened in the middle of the night to see where things in the sky had moved; to see what new stars were appearing. There were no bugs, no clouds, no sounds, and just an occasional breeze as the cool nighttime air covered over us like a blanket of peace. I wondered how I could create this in my daily life, this peace and calmness, without becoming bored.

The last morning we piled back into the jeep and set off for Acraba, where all of us would go in different directions. I was saddened to say goodbye to my new friends, because being with them had been one of those precious times when the stars and planets aligned and magic happened between people. Waving goodbye as my last companion stepped into a taxi, I was alone again—but this time, wishing I wasn't.

Such is travel. Things would soon change, as I was about to visit many friends in Israel that I had met while traveling.

Indiana Jones move over photographs   [95], page 141   [96], page 141   [97], page 141

Entry Forty-two: Thank You, Israel

I completely underestimated the enormous historical, political and theological significance of Israel. I was overwhelmed as it began to sink in that I was in one of the most complex places in the world. Since I was still processing what I had experienced in other places, my trip to Israel was surely going to offer me even more to chew on.

I knew from the beginning I would be coming to Israel, but I hadn't mentioned it too much. I hadn't wanted to worry those people who were already worried about my travels. Still, it was unthinkable for me to plan a large trip abroad without going to the Holy Land. Inside its borders lay some of the most sacred places known to mankind. In addition, I had met in my travels many living in Israel who had invited me to come visit, and that was a good sign.

My border crossing from Jordan was to be a telling story of what lay ahead of me in Israel, although I didn't know it at the time. Normally a busy crossing, I walked alone in the ghosttown-like border area that connected Israel to Jordan. The place was completely deserted so I read my book as I waited for someone to come stamp my passport, allowing me to leave Jordan. Finally someone did show up, smiles were exchanged, and he wished me well as I walked across the empty space between checkpoints.

The corridor was lined with a chain link fence on both sides. On the fences were red and white signs warning all not to leave the pathway because of mine fields. Hmmm, not the place to go play.

I had been coached by my friends from Israel that my arrival in their country would most likely be greeted by a million questions from security personnel. And they were correct. The lady attending me asked where I was going and, specifically, what I intended to see and whom I intended to meet.

Thankfully, I had read the guidebook a little the night before and had gotten a couple of ideas, like Jerusalem and Bethlehem. It got trickier when she wanted specifics, but with a sincere face I stated that I'd only just read the guidebook the night before. I told her that I was going to see first-hand what was there. She smiled and apologized for asking me so many questions. But since she was a nice young woman, in nice-fitting jeans and somewhat attractive, I didn't mind.

After a thorough search of my bag and having reached the end of all the questions, I was told to leave, with a smile and a "Welcome to Israel."

The moment I crossed the border there was a different intensity in the wind. It was as if someone had plugged the atmosphere into an electrical socket so that each breath I took had a buzzing, sharp edge to it. I noticed this long before I arrived at the bus station where I discovered a terminal full of teenaged machine gun-toting soldiers on their way to somewhere. But that didn't bother me. I wondered to myself as I looked across the bus aisle at the guy with his AK47, whether I had been traveling too long since I wasn't disturbed by such a sight.

I arrived in Tel Aviv and started calling those I knew, making an attempt to allocate time and create some kind of plan. First I called Stan, then Tamar, Neta, Moran, Itamar, Nomai, and Maya.

There were a few others that I didn't get called. It was nothing personal. It was just that I was overwhelmed with so many people pulling on me after being a lone traveler for so long. To those people I apologize, and hope you understand. I was caught between being a lone traveler and visiting family. This created some internal tension that rises from the difference. But after a little time of studying the map and beginning to comprehend where people lived, a plan started to come together.

And I would also be remiss if I forgot to acknowledge that Neta took it upon herself to be my tour planner. After a couple days of visiting people and exploring Tel Aviv, I headed for Jerusalem, Israel's spiritual heart, and for many, the holiest city of all. Moving from the modern metropolitan city of Tel Aviv to the ancient and walled city of Jerusalem was more than just moving back in time. It was as if God himself had picked me up by the collar and dropped me into the middle of this incomprehensible maze of energy and feelings. This city was connected together by narrow, winding streets that had invisible barriers allowing only certain souls to pass.

Jerusalem is a mass of sacred, holy places that one could spend a lifetime exploring, and some do. I had two days. My list had three top priorities: first was the Church of the Holy Sepulchre, which is the site where Jesus was crucified, buried and resurrected. Next was the Western Wall, which is the only remaining physical evidence of what was once the Jews' holiest ancient building. It's now an open-air synagogue. And finally, I wanted to see the Temple Mount and Dome of the Rock. This site, according to Islam, is heaven on earth where Mohammed launched himself to the heavens. This last place was off-limits due to current tensions, so I let it go for another trip or another lifetime. The other two I visited several times, at various times of the day and night.

It was here, as I walked through connecting corridors, I rediscovered and nurtured my amazement of mankind's ongoing struggle to express his relationship with the Divine. For there is no other place in the world where so much means so many different things to so many people. And in this timeless setting, the countless spirits have left their imprints on the rocks and stones used to construct and reconstruct this holy city called Jerusalem. This place vibrates with its own unique rhythm in such a profound magnitude that it is impossible not to be brought to your knees in humility.

My first destination was the Church of the Holy Sepulchre. It was the first of several visits here, as I slowly began to appreciate where I actually was. The structure itself is an unorganized mess of rooms and attachments belonging to various churches of the Christian faith. It was by pure luck that I showed up as the Catholics held their daily 4 PM service, walking through the church singing their Gregorian-type chants. It gave the place a sense of reverence as the saintly voices echoed through the stone chambers.

I followed them around the complex as they went from sacred place to sacred place and offered my own silent voice that sang its own song of gratitude and praise in my heart. For in me has always lived an unshakeable love for the Son of God known as Jesus. To be here in this place was bringing my own faith and history to life as expressed in the physical world. No longer were the Bible stories only stories. I could touch, feel and smell the very places where Jesus once walked and lived.

And it was with deep reverence that I offered my prayers of gratitude, not unlike the many other prayers I offered at the multitude of shrines for different religions as I traveled along my journey. For with them all, I have approached these places with deepest love that knows no color, no language and no time. It is only this purest love from the soul that makes us all part of the same humanity.

Inside the church there is a tomb where the body of Jesus had been laid. It is a small stone structure with a tiny doorway leading into another small room. This room has an even tinier door opening into a very small room. It is in this last small room where the body of Jesus had been laid. As I waited to enter the room, I silently touched the stone walls to feel chiseled carvings and reminded myself that I was here, and not just dreaming. There were few people around. This allowed me to have the space and time to enter the sacred room at my own pace. When I finally did enter the room, I knew I was in a place like no other. As I knelt there, with folded hands resting on the stone, I knew I had come to a place that had been waiting for me for a long time. As I knelt there, first my arms and then my entire body felt as if I had stuck my hand into an electrical socket. It didn't startle me, for I was aware of its divine nature and allowed it to reach in and touch my soul.

When I was finished, I then went to the place where the crucifixion took place, and knelt before the altar. While there I lit a candle of gratitude and prayed for my Grandmother whose endless prayers follow me everywhere, and for my family and friends who have given me so much. I prayed for my guardian angels that I have been blessed with for protection, and for all who have shared their hearts with me, touching me so. I prayed for all who have come before me, all who were there now, and all who will come after me in this place. My prayer was that peace be in their hearts always.

After three hours of sitting in the church, I went for a walk. I wandered through the streets until I found myself in front of the Western Wall. The wall is the only remaining part of the once grand Jewish Temple that, according to those who know, was filled with the Divine Presence. I had heard so much of this place, but knew so little about it. I sat in this sacred place and absorbed the passionate air, becoming almost intoxicated by the richness of such devotion. This too was an unforgettable scene: the full moon rose above the great wall that was illumined by lights, with men and women leaning against it in prayer.

Not knowing the history of such places can limit the depth of appreciation of the moment. I felt in myself a hunger to know and understand more of the scene before me, but had to trust it would reveal itself over time. My main responsibility at this point was to be as aware as possible of the nature of this special place.

In the evenings, I worked my way back to Moran's home by local bus. She lived with her parents outside of Jerusalem. Like every home I visited, they stuffed me with food and gracious hospitality. The bus rides were always an experience in themselves, as each person was eyed as they stepped onto the bus by the other travelers. The sad scenes of suicide bombers have taken their toll on the spirits of those who ride the bus. It showed in the eyes of the passengers trying to live their ordinary lives. Even more sadly, it doesn't appear to be changing anytime soon.

After Jerusalem, I made a trip to Bethlehem, the birthplace of Jesus, in the Palestinian Territory. The understanding of the location didn't come for me until later. I climbed into a minibus as directed by my travel guide and eventually enough people climbed on so we could make the trip.

As we traveled down the road, I remember thinking to myself, "Wow, this road is small." The impression I had from looking at the map was that it was a real highway. We bounced along for a while, and then suddenly turned off into an olive grove. We wound our way through the orchard as branches brushed against the sides of the bus. "Wow," I thought, "this is just like India." I didn't think much more about it.

Arriving in Bethlehem the driver stopped, pointed upward and said "Church, church." I jumped out and walked on up to the church. There I found a deserted parking lot in front of a huge church. The Church of the Nativity is a citadel over the cave where it is believed that Jesus was born. I entered the huge structure by a door so small that I was required to stoop to walk through it, like an enforced act of humility. The church was completely empty except for a few clergy walking about.

A local man followed me around, and I ended up hiring him as a guide to explain things. He paraded me through the different areas of the church, explaining things that I would have missed otherwise. We went to the Catholic area where the Christmas Eve mass is broadcast worldwide each year. He pointed out the bullet holes in the walls, leftover remnants of the siege of April 2000. Below in the cave, he explained, was where the manger, the actual birthplace of Jesus, was located.

After my tour, I wandered back to this place. I sat alone in quietness and solitude, half-giddy and half-sad. I kept thinking about my Lutheran pastors and how they probably would have loved to trade places with me at this moment. This place normally has a two-to-three hour-long line waiting to get to this point where I sat alone for an hour, having my own internal dialog and prayer. For all those pastors I gave a prayer of thanks. Before leaving, I took out of my pocket a cross that I had purchased in Jerusalem for my Grandmother, and laid it on the stone that marked the birthplace of Jesus.

After a few moments, I left the cave for the last time and went outside to figure out how to get home. While talking with my guide again, he asked how my border crossing had been coming in. It was then that I realized that we didn't come across any border crossing. Instead the minibus had sneaked us in through some back way, and now I was in the Palestinian Territory. So I headed for the proper border crossing. On my way, I walked past boarded-up houses and storefronts. The area had a deserted, eerie feeling to it that revealed some of the ongoing struggles between these two nations. Crossing the border was easy as an American. Afterwards I hopped onto a bus back to Moran's.

My last day of exploring was spent at the Dead Sea where I conducted my own experiments of sitting on top of this strange water. The lowest place on earth at 410 meters below sea level, this place is like no other. As waves rolled in, I bobbed up and down like a bobber a few yards offshore in the clear salty sea. Rocks along the shore were coated with white salt crystals. Deposited from some former wave, they had since dried into sparkles glistening in the sun. After a shower, I went inland to hike up to David Falls, enjoying the solitude of nature and the uniqueness of a stream in the desert.

I said goodbye to Moran and her family, then shot back to Tel Aviv to join Neta for a trip to the Golan Heights to visit her aunt and uncle. I enjoyed the ride and the freedom of being in a car that could move where we wanted. We arrived at the farm in the late afternoon, after a little side trip of being lost—but no lost time as it showed us some unexpected scenery. Once again I was treated to some amazing home cooking, the likes of which I've never known. I felt like I was beginning to make up for some of my former weight loss.

The Golan Heights of upper Israel are beautiful, lush and peaceful. It is a place where the soul can go "ahhhhhh" and relax for a moment. Looking down on the Sea of Galilee I could see the entire vista where Jesus once preached and performed various miracles. My hosts were kind in showing me around the area. This even included a nighttime wildlife-spotlighting trip that reminded me of Nebraska days long gone when I would go raccoon hunting with my friend, Curt. (Except in Golan, the only thing I had to shoot with was a camera.)

The next day we toured around the various Christian holy places, including the site of the Sermon on the Mount. They dropped me off in Nazareth where I spent a night sleeping in a convent of French nuns. After Nazareth I headed to Haifa to meet my friend Itamar, whom I had met in Australia. We sat around for a couple of days, catching up on life and discussing issues like women, over beer. Then it was back to Tel Aviv to finish off my whirlwind trip and say goodbye.

While in Israel I spent a great deal of time listening to the various interpretations and opinions of the issues at hand. The intensity and depth of listening was helpful to begin, and I stress *begin*, to gain some understanding of this place. It also made me tired, and I felt it was time to move on to Egypt. Israel is truly a complex and amazing place. I will be eternally grateful to all those who offered such gracious hospitality.

There are so many friends and relatives who were so kind:

Stan,   I thank you for the chats about matters of Israel and the heart.

Miss Neta,   thank you for sharing your friends and family with me, feeding me so well and taking such good care of me, plus exposing me to the Irish Pub.

Tamar,   I thank you for meeting me on my first night in Israel and welcoming me.

Moran,   I thank you for sharing your family with me, and the insightful palm reading.

Itamar,   the chats were great, and the topic one of my favorites.

Namio,   your sweetness and depth of heart still rules.

Maya,   thank you for your calm wisdom and the rakee treatment.

This list is way too short to cover how I feel, but you get the idea. One of the best quotes I heard on my trip came from Neta's mom: "If I were young again, I'd make more mistakes."

So I was off to make more mistakes and see where they might lead me.

Thank you, Israel photographs   [98], page 142   [99], page 143   [100], page 143
     [101], page 143   [102], page 143   [103], page 144

Entry Forty-three: Behold the pyramids

After traveling one month in Egypt, I felt it was time to be on my way to the next place.

The time in Egypt was a series of daily ups and downs as I navigated through that maze of a culture. Arriving on the coast of the Red Sea, I crashed for ten days—resting, reading, and enjoying the empty schedule of my lifestyle. The Red Sea has amazing water for snorkeling and diving. The water is clear, filled with endless colorful fish, and all right at your doorstep.

After my R&R on the coast, I scooted up to St. Katherine's monastery, where I spent an afternoon climbing Mt. Sinai. Most people watch the sunrise from the top of the mountain; I chose to watch the sunset because it offered the chance to be alone. I sat there watching the sun sink into the Sinai desert, having my own internal dialog without a burning bush, but no less important for me.

From Sinai I headed for Cairo, the full-on, polluted city with the slickest touts (hawkers) I'd yet encountered. I had one goal for myself while in Egypt, and that was to see the pyramids. The main pyramids lay just outside of Cairo in a place called Giza. They were located right on the edge of a large city, unlike my mind's picture of them being in the middle of the desert. I arrived at the pyramids early in the morning, ahead of the busloads of tourists, and had the place pretty much to myself.

The pyramids constitute one of the oldest tourist attractions in the world. Thousands of years old, there's not much else to say that hasn't already been said. So let me simply add this: "Wow!" I climbed inside the largest pyramid and spent some time alone in the main chamber where they laid the dead pharaoh. The dark stone room had a different feel to it, a different vibration, maybe all in my head; the energy was turned up a little. The pyramids were built as a causeway to eternity for the pharaohs. It's a nice idea, anyway.

Walking around the pyramids, you are constantly bombarded with offers for camel rides, horse rides, and special access to rooms for a little extra baksheesh (money). It can wear you down if you let it. This is Egypt; every place where a tourist might go, you will find someone willing to help you spend your money. Generally they'll tell you almost anything that might increase the chances of your money becoming theirs.

Once while I was in Luxor, I hired a bike for a day to go see the Valley of the Kings. The valley was on the other side of the Nile, which meant I would have to take a ferry to cross over to the other side. While looking for the public ferry, several touts approached me claiming that the ferry was down below. As I approached the public ferry, the last tout tried a last ditch effort claiming he had the ferry. When I informed him that the ferry was right down below, he then said that they didn't allow bicycles on the boat. I looked at him and said, "You're lying." He just smiled and walked away.

It was this ability to lie with such ease that frustrated me so, or the constant asking of money or pens from everyone: police, touts, beggars—all attempting to get a piece of my pie. Then when I would least expect it, someone would do something for me out of pure kindness and rekindle my faith in humanity. Thus the cycle of ups and downs would continue.

After exploring the pyramids, I headed south to Aswan and Luxor to explore the majestic ruins of the Egyptian civilization and for my felucca ride down the Nile. Sailing down the Nile was one of the highlights of my trip through Egypt. No touts, no horns, no pollution—just wind, blue skies and nighttime stars. For two days and nights we lived on the boat, following the current of the mighty Nile. As I lay on the boat deck, I reached over the edge and dipped my hands into the cool, clear water. This river is so rich in history, when you touch its waters you touch the endless generations it has fed, and the numerous pharaohs who have traversed over its surface.

The Nile asks for nothing, yet it gives to those who ask. This corridor of an oasis, a strip of green cutting through sand and stone, creates a striking contrast for the eyes. It nourishes the soul, bringing forth life from the heart of Africa as it races to the sea. This floating delight ended in Luxor, where I spent the remainder of my time exploring tombs and temples. My favorite was Karnak. This massive structure, with its incredible carvings telling the stories of days gone by, left me wondering what future generations will have to look at from our time here. Do we build anything now that will last 4,000 years? Does anyone really care?

On a fascinating note, one of my roommates at the Dahab Hotel in downtown Cairo was a young man from Canada, Kory French. Kory had been traveling for a long time, and through several of the same places as myself. We thought it was funny that we hadn't crossed paths before. Three days had gone by and one night we were sitting down for dinner in a Chinese restaurant, and next to us was a table full of loud Americans. This triggered a memory for Kory, and he started to tell me a story of an American he had met in Vietnam. Then he stopped and asked me several questions. It was strange, as we both became aware that the story he was about to tell was about me.

We were both on the same tour of the DMZ zone when a busload of Americans showed up and I chewed out this woman for being so rude and insensitive at the war museum. He went on to explain how he had told that story over and over about this American who said what everyone else wanted to say to this stupid woman, but felt they couldn't because they weren't from America. It was a bizarre experience to have a re-encounter with someone from a moment, impacting as it was, that felt like such a long time ago.

We celebrated the reunion with a farewell party for Kory; he was going home to Canada after traveling for two and a half years. Watching Kory prepare and pack brought the reality home to me that the day would come soon when I would pack my own bag not for a new country, but for the place most familiar to me: my home.

On a sad note, I received some bad news from home that a dear uncle of mine had died in a farming accident. It sent me into a shock for several days and drove home the fact that I was far from home. While walking down the street after having just read that news, a tout came up to me trying some of his tactics. I waved him off, not having the energy to deal with him. He then started yelling at me, "You're a Jew, aren't you?" Then he started spitting at me and calling me names. "Jeesh," I thought, "we're in trouble as a world."

In another encounter, I had the opportunity to dialogue with a couple of young Islamic women. I was probing in an attempt to understand more about Islam. Two things in this encounter struck me. First, they were sincere and sweet in their willingness to discuss things. Second, when I asked them why Muslims hated Jews so much, a fiery hatred filled their eyes as they went on about how evil the Jews were, killing innocent women and children.

They then presented their own belief that it was Israel who masterminded the twin tower attacks so America would strike against Islam. I thought to myself, "The truth is getting lost in the piles of propaganda from both sides." I fear now, as I did that day, that this is leading to a dangerous situation that will never lead to peace, only more needless suffering.

My favorite time of the day was 5 PM. It was Ramadan, the fasting month for Islam, when I visited Egypt. The Muslims do not eat, drink or do anything fun during daylight hours. Once 5 PM hits, the day is over and they have what they call breakfast. It is a wonderful moment, because even in the heart of downtown Cairo, everything comes to a halt for 30 minutes as all the Muslims stop to eat. The city turns into a ghost town. I can walk down the middle of what just moments before were the busiest streets and not see one car. Along the roadsides I saw very long tables filled with Muslims as they sat together eating for the first time since before dawn. It was a rare, peaceful moment that I cherished.

My mind kept pushing away the news about Uncle Frank, and our family surely gathered around his in Villisca, Iowa. I didn't want to believe it was true, but the pain in my heart told me something different. As the train rolled its way south, I looked around and discovered I was the only person in the entire passenger car. The blackness of night passed by with an occasional nighttime light on the horizon.

I pulled my feet up onto the seat and sat in my prayerful position. As the tears flowed down my cheeks, I searched my heart for answers. The only one that gave me any peace was this: God must have acquired some new land, and was looking for a good man to farm it. In that search he found a man who had done a good job of feeding His children and decided to bring him home to feed His angels, to sow the rich soils of heaven, where the crops are always a bumper, the rains always soft, and the sunshine always perfect.

I dedicate this chapter to my Uncle Frank, a man I always admired and will always love. His humility and inner strength will always serve as an example of how to live life. He made me proud to be a part of the Jacobs family.

Next is Ethiopia.

Behold the pyramids photographs [104], page 144 [105], page 144 [106], page 145

[107], page 145 [108], page 145 [109], page 146

Entry Forty-Four: A short note from Addis

I flew to Ethiopia. At one point I had seriously considered going overland through the Sudan, and really wanted to. There was one small problem that ended the debate in my mind: I had an Israeli stamp in my passport, and with that stamp in my passport, the Sudanese government would not allow me to enter. What a shame, because I was hearing reports of nice people and interesting experiences. It will wait for another day, but not another lifetime.

Not long after my arrival in Addis Ababa (the Ethiopian capital), I found myself stuck in a pizzeria joint with a bottle of Highland Queen Scotch Whiskey before me—filled with tap water. It gave the scene a manly image, a sense of Hemingway. My notebook was sprawled out before me; various guide books scattered across the tabletop. My hat hung on the corner of the empty chair that sat across from me. The only thing missing was an ashtray with a lit cigarette sending up smoke signals. To top it all, I was half-shaven. Truly, I projected the image of the rugged traveler.

Except my head wasn't cloudy from alcohol. Instead, it was cloudy from the head cold that had flattened me out and prevented me from exploring further afield. I wasn't willing to continue until my body was stronger, so I waited a few days in Addis before moving on. Of the few reports I'd heard from other travelers in Ethiopia, the same message kept coming: it's rough travel.

I registered with the U.S. embassy, more out of boredom than concern, and when I told the nice woman where I was intending to go she just gave me one of those motherly looks and told me to be careful. She informed me that the average wage in Ethiopia is $115 a year.

On the way back to my hotel, I had the cab stop by the Hilton Hotel. I wanted to pick up a phrase book from their bookstore, so I could try and communicate more with the locals. I stopped by the front desk and out of curiosity asked what a night cost. She said $175. I wondered how that's explained to people here, and at the same time I had my own fantasy of checking in and ditching my $3 a night room. But that day was—and still is—yet to come.

Stopping by the Hilton was like stepping into a different world. Clean and orderly, a large decorated Christmas tree sat in the middle of the lobby. It reminded me that, back home, there were countless trees with presents underneath. For a moment I was homesick for family, friends, for work that gave challenge and personal meaning. I daydreamed for a moment about being back home, then sent those thoughts home in the form of a prayer.

Entry Forty-Five: It's a different way of life

When I landed in Ethiopia, I really landed—flat on my back. Thank God for music. Otherwise I would have gone crazy lying there in my bed, too lightheaded to read and too restless to sleep. But after nine days, I was healthy enough to begin traveling. That was good, because I was really getting bored in Addis. Addis is nothing special, so I was particularly happy to finally be on my way. It was challenging to navigate with so many people begging and needing so much. But, unlike India, here there's more of a sense of aggression and frustration combined with the poverty. This leads to more tricky situations and potential dangers.

Ethiopia has its challenges. It's one of the poorest nations in the world. According to a Swedish medical student I met, 40% of the population lives further than a one-day walk from the nearest road. The average income there is $115 a year, and all the problems that brings. But it is rich in cultural history, natural beauty and charming people.

You have the extremes happening all at once in Addis. One day on the way back from the bank I stopped a pickpocket scam, became stirred up by the incident and made myself "ready for battle." Then 20 minutes later, a car stopped for me as I walked along with my backpack and offered me a free ride across town. I was once again melted by the kindness of those who have so little.

Originally my plan was to go to northern Ethiopia, but my nine days in bed forced me to scratch that plan. Instead I began heading south; those treasures of the north will have to wait for another day. I went through the more remote parts of the country. As we bounced down the potholed roads that eventually turned to dirt and rock, the scene outside was a moving time machine. The further away from Addis we went, the more incredible the scene became.

Dirt paths and thatched houses replaced concrete roads and buildings. Rural pedestrians replaced cars and bicycles. This is one of the sights I was so stricken by in Ethiopia: streets and roads filled with people walking, sometimes way out in what looks like the middle of nowhere. Even in the smaller towns and villages there are few vehicles, so people use the oldest form of transportation: two legs.

I was the only white person aboard the bus, but never felt any judgments or discrimination, only curious eyes and questions. The only discrimination I had to encounter came from shop owners, restaurants and sometimes hotels who tried to charge me double the price for things because I had white skin. That's the way it was from the day I left Australia, so it was nothing new.

I lost track of the number of beautiful birds we passed on the way. My biology training left me wishing for a field guide, because without one, I was lost. So I had to settle back and simply enjoy seeing such an abundance of wildlife.

The parts of Ethiopia I explored on my way to Kenya were the mountains. They provided a total contrast to the image of a flat brown desert I had always associated with Ethiopia. Instead, we passed valley after plush green valley as we headed south for the Omo Valley.

Eventually I got to the end of the road, Jinka, but not before we'd passed numerous people roadside that were living as they had for countless generations. I'm at a loss for words to describe the scenes of farmers and hunters still carrying spears, using animal skins for clothing or backpacks. They used gourds for water jugs, and often went without shoes.

While in Jinka, I went to a couple of local markets that served people from the surrounding area. It was intense for me to be in the middle of a scene from the daily life of so many tribal people. It was a bit intimidating at one point— only because it was so different, so raw, so basic, and yet so beautiful. I'm no anthropologist, but I wished for someone there to explain the marketplace sight to me so I could have a deeper understanding of its significance. I had to settle for an intellectual surrender to what looks like uncivilized society one moment, then a dignified social structure the next. These amazing people still live a life that allows them to radiate a smile that can light up the sky.

While exploring I was "adopted" by an Ethiopian group from a cement company who were on a company tour. They were a warm and generous group, and they watched over me like family. On the outside of their bus they had a speaker connected to the music system that would play the music outside as we went down the road. It was unforgettable to see the children dance as they heard the music passing by—and not only the children, but also adults. "How does that happen?" I thought. "Some places in the world hear noise, while others hear music that makes them want to dance."

After touring around the Omo Valley, I caught a ride with a truck heading south towards the Kenya border. It was one of those moments that I knew I was exactly where I was supposed to be. Standing in the back of that truck, with the wind blowing across my face and through my hair, I smiled the big smile of a happy heart. I watched the beauty of a distant rain cloud with a long tail of gray rain underneath, red dirt roads leading to unseen villages, hills, valleys and empty grass plains with solitary trees. Colorfully dressed people would pop up roadside, waving madly in attempts to get a ride, but the truck wouldn't stop and just kept rolling along.

I was left with an unmistakable sense of freedom; that the world was a gift for me to explore. It was being rolled out before me like a buffet table and I was given the chance to sample a small taste of the delicacy for that day. For this I gave thanks.

Ethiopia is a country with intimacy and dignity. Over and over I enjoyed meeting people, observing their interactions with me and with one another. The greeting process was quite elaborate, depending on the type of relationship. But even to strangers, a bow slightly forward was offered along with a handshake. I liked it; it seemed to give honor to the exchange while it broke down barriers.

The other experience that touched me was when it was time to eat, many times I was invited to join people, no matter how little they had. In addition, I ate from the same plate as they did, and by hand. At first it felt strange and uncomfortable, but after a while I loved it, because it created a real intimacy between people. They would put piles of food on top of what I can only describe as a huge sourdough pancake. I tore off pieces for myself and scooped up the other goodies with it. Many times the best bites were given to me, and sometimes even fed directly into my mouth.

You can only let go and dive in at these moments, otherwise you miss out. I learned a different type of intimacy with them, and I took that with me.

My ride from the border town of Moyale to Nairobi turned out to be a cattle truck. In this part of the country there are no buses. I opted for the front seat, although I had to pay double (the foreigner price). But given the rain at the time, I was willing to fork over a few more dollars. A seat up front rather than riding on top of the racks above the cattle seemed like a smart move at the moment.

The rain, however, was a bad sign. One-third of the way into our journey to Nairobi, we ran into mud roads unlike anything I've ever seen before. We would move ten yards, get stuck for ten minutes, move 50 yards and get stuck again. At one point we got really stuck, and I decided to go for a walk up the road thinking, "This is going to take some time." So off alone I trotted. Up ahead was a woman—a fellow passenger who had been riding on top— with a baby strapped to her back who also decided to walk on ahead.

After walking for almost an hour, I turned back around. I couldn't hear the truck any more and was getting a little concerned. Yet I loved the solitude of the empty road and the quiet it offered.

At one point three soldiers appeared, carrying machine guns and sporting grenades wrapped around their waists. I thought they were from my truck and had come to find me. Then the one that could speak English asked me where my car was.

Obviously, they weren't from my truck. Then the spokesman proceeded to tell me not to be afraid; they weren't like some fighters who robbed people along the road. He went on to explain his cause. They were Liberation Freedom Fighters of something or another. His parents had been killed along with many others in his village. He said that they only asked for support. I thought, "How much— $50 or $100?" But he wanted only moral support. They were fighting for land, not robbing people for money.

Eventually we came close to the truck. The three freedom fighters asked me if there were armed guards. I told them I had no idea, so they disappeared after we shook hands and said goodbye. I walked back to the truck and started shoveling mud.

A few minutes later, the three freedom fighters appeared. Everyone became very quiet. Tension filled the air. I blurted out, "Hello, it's my friends!" They smiled at me as they walked by, and went on their way. The passengers of the truck laughed as their fear of being robbed passed. Then they became really curious about me, the man who made friends with freedom fighters. They later shared about how they were worried about me as I strolled off alone down the road. They said, "It very dangerous here." I told them I didn't know I was supposed to be afraid.

From that point forward, though, I stayed close to the truck.

That first night was a long one. We spent most of the night stuck in the mud, making slow progress. The rain stopped. At one point I found a small place along the road that was a little drier than the other muddy parts, and fell asleep for 30 minutes. I lay on the road next to a local man who was a policeman going home to see his family.

Looking up at the star-filled sky, I asked him about his family. He talked about his son, who was crazy about riding his bicycle wherever and whenever he could. He shared about his wife, whom he had met at school. He spoke about his anticipation of seeing them after being away for four months. I listened, and thought about my own family and friends and felt the same way about the day when I would see them again.

As I trailed off into sleep, I thought about pleasant things, like Paris in the springtime, hot mashed potatoes, wearing jeans again, reading stories to my grandmother, and playing with my nieces and nephews.

On day four of the three-day trip, we finally pulled into Nairobi. The last ten miles were very interesting; every half-mile there was a police check. Sometimes the checkpoints were so close that, while you were stopped, you could see the next one down the road. They were racking up the money, charging all the trucks that went through, and any other car they felt like stopping.

It was a more refined type of robbery, I thought, as the driver complained to me in detail how corrupt the police were. He also mentioned his hope that the election might bring in a less corrupt government. It was election time in Kenya, and for the first time in 20 years, people believed there was the real possibility the election wasn't rigged.

It was a potentially tricky time in Nairobi. If something bad did go down, I would be stuck in the middle of it all. Nothing bad happened, it seemed. I was able to see a peaceful election. I was hopeful for the people of Kenya. Maybe corruption was finally being addressed, somehow.

Entry Forty-six: *Safari*

Another forgotten dream: Africa. But in retrospect, I had not completely forgotten the dream—just covered it over with so many ideas of what I thought life was supposed to look like, instead of consulting my own heart for answers. I mean, who doesn't, as a child, dream of an African safari?

The safari of Africa is breathtaking. It is impossible, no matter how much money you have for production (i.e. Disney), to duplicate the scene before your eyes. The sheer magnitude and abundance of wildlife is beyond words. It is a place of timeless change and remembrance.

It truly was a dream come true for me to finally get to see such amazing, beautiful and majestic animals roaming freely. It inspires the soul, and touches those inner spaces that yearn for such freedom. Zoos have often left me feeling a bit sad. Africa had the opposite effect, and left me with such a high that it will forever be etched into my spirit.

Watching a large herd of giraffes walking on a distant hillside completely stopped me in my tracks, and filled me with awe. Their long necks stretched high into the sky. As they gracefully glided across the green backdrop, it was like being transported to a dream where they once set the rules for life and death. It is testimony to how straightforward the cycles of life can be. You live, you eat, you hunt, you kill, you hide and you run away. Sometimes there isn't much more to say, and all you can do is smile.

We drove around the game parks for three days. This gave me the opportunity to see elephants, giraffes, zebras, lions, cheetahs, rhinos, gazelles, baboons, countless types of birds and three million flamingos on Lake Nakuru. This time I was the one in the cage, and preferred it that way. I wasn't ready to become an hors d'oeuvre for some lion. I opted for the plastic seat and pop-up rooftop. Besides, the last time I went for a walk, I soon discovered that almost everything has thorns and sharp leaves. Why do such harsh environments always have nasty plants? It's like God is saying, "Stay away, unless you like having more problems!"

As a part of the safari, we made a stop at a local Masai village. The Masai are an indigenous people whose culture has resisted change. They still live a different and colorful life that leaves me thankful that I was born in the U.S. It brought up the same questions that have haunted me for some time: "How does a soul get born into this situation? What can I learn from it all?" There's so much to learn and so little time.

It was good to be out of Nairobi, or "Nairobbery" as they call it. It's not a fun place to explore. The only thing that saved me was meeting Buck at the Christmas Eve service I attended. Buck was a US Aid government worker who graciously opened his home to me, which gave me access to a hot shower and a real washing machine. We spent a day together driving around a part of Nairobi, and did some shopping. It gave me a glimpse of what life looks like for the ex-pats, very different from the area where I was staying, downtown in Scarysville.

As we drove around that day, we passed the area where the new Kenyan president was being sworn in. The streets were filled with jubilant people, carrying signs and branches from trees, chanting and singing songs in celebration of the victory. It was an amazing sight, and had this borderline mob energy. I was careful to make the hand signal of the winning party, a peace sign.

I must admit that it was unplanned timing on my part to be in Kenya for the elections. It was when I reached the border with Ethiopia that I discovered Kenya was about to have elections. It was even later that I learned that past elections had been scarred by great violence and demonstrations, a result of corruption in the election process. Thankfully, I got to witness a peaceful transition of governments in Kenya. The mood was very upbeat and optimistic about corruption being dealt with, so ordinary people might have a chance to prosper. It is the first time in many years that they have been given some hope; let us also hope for them, for a bright and fair future.

Christmas in Nairobi was different than in Thailand. The service was in English this time; there was no lottery drawing, but it was nice to be in a place that celebrated Christmas.

After running around Nairobi for the day and enjoying a wonderful dinner, I said goodbye to Buck. The next day I bolted off for Tanzania, to find a way to explore more safari and more adventure.

As I bounced down the road in northern Kenya, the radio played a sentimental song that fit the scene. With the bush of the Kenya landscape, colorful tribal people walking roadside and the occasional wild beast, I listened to the radio play "I'll Be Home for Christmas." And true enough, "...if only in my dreams." It was all a part of the adventure, the journey and missing family and friends for the holidays.

Safari photographs

[116], page 149 [117], page 149 [118], page 150
[119], page 150 [120], page 150

Entry Forty-seven: Tanzanian wow

After crossing the border into Tanzania, I jumped off the bus in Arusha.

Arusha is a hub town filled with countless safari companies all scrambling for your business (which, for the tourist/traveler, translates into pain in the butt). But I was so happy to be out of Nairobi that I didn't care.

After some research, I opted to join a five-day safari to see the Serengeti and Ngorongoro Crater. The Serengeti has a vastness that is nothing short of stunning. The open plains were green and lush from recent rains. The gray dirt roads were muddy and tricky to drive on at times.

"Serengeti" is a Masai term that roughly translates into "the grass that goes forever." And that it does. As we bounced down the dirt road in our four-wheel drive, it seemed to never end. It was as close as you can come to seeing a visual of the infinite, or actually seeing a physical picture of forever. As a sea of green grass expanded before your eyes, you would encounter not a single animal for miles. Then, slowly, silhouettes would start to appear on the horizon, and as they got larger they would be replaced by even more silhouettes, until as far as you could see there was nothing but wildlife to overwhelm the senses. The sheer mass of wildlife was staggering.

The reality of life sets in fast, too. If there is any romantic idea of this place, it disappears as you watch a group of hyenas tear apart a gazelle. The initial euphoria of seeing wild animals had begun in Kenya. But the magic spell of being in the middle of the endless Serengeti wove its own special sort of inspiration.

Our guide said we were lucky. Here's why: Driving down the road we approached a lioness walking ahead of us. As we approached her, she left the road and climbed up a short embankment. When she did this it gave her a view of what we could already see: a family of warthogs mucking around in the grass.

Instantly, the lioness crouched down to the ground and slowly began to work her way around to one side of the warthogs. She moved into a new spot to avoid being upwind of the prey. She inched closer, until she was close enough to chase and kill both of the young ones. Breaking and strangling the neck of the first one swiftly, she dropped it and gave chase to the second. Pouncing around the grass, she quickly caught the second and dinner was served.

It was so fast and lethal that I had to replay it over in my mind several times to simply comprehend what I'd just watched. We might have been lucky, but the warthogs weren't. It left no doubt in regard to the power and swiftness of lions, and smashed any foolish daydreamy idea of trying to outrun one to the car.

The nights were especially impressive. I lay there in my tent at night in my sleeping bag, listening to all makes of strange noises. Lions roaring, elephants trumpeting, the sounds of flamingos drifting up from the lake below; it brought back all of those scary childhood fears of not wanting to look under the bed, or in this case, to peek outside the tent.

With only a nylon tent separating me from the chance of becoming someone's midnight snack, I loved it. If we allow it, nature can teach us what's really important in the most basic ways. These simple lessons are a tool that has been used throughout the ages in the lessons of life. It is for this reason we must be good stewards of the land. Once lost, it's gone forever.

After three days in the Serengeti, we spent a full day in the Ngorongoro Crater. Reportedly hosting the highest concentration of large game wildlife in the world, it did not disappoint. The descent into the crater did, however, feel a little zoo-like after roaming the open plains of the Serengeti. Inside the crater we saw rhinos, elephants, hyenas, zebras, lions, jackals, countless types of birds, gazelles, and probably a few things I can't remember now.

This was all punctuated by a lunchtime break where several kites (a type of hawk-like bird) flew down and grabbed the food right out of two of my ride mates' hands, and left a scratch mark on my hand with their attempt to get my lunch, too. "Yep, Disney can't do that one," I thought. "Too many lawsuits otherwise."

Eventually the safari came to an end. The last hour, for fun, I became the driver of our jeep, and found a whole new respect for those who have to drive on those crappy roads. It was good to drive again, anyway. I even started to point out and spot things as we went down the road. They told me I could get a job if I wanted. Hey, maybe that's it! (Nah.)

I spent one more night in Arusha, and then headed to Moshi the next day. Moshi sits at the base of Mt. Kilimanjaro. All I wanted was to see it. The cost to climb it was just too much at $600 for the cheaper treks. I decided to use that money to see other things, or save the climbing for Nepal and back in the States.

After my sunrise view from the bottom of Kili, I headed for Dar es Salaam and made plans to keep going south. Well, actually west and south to Zambia and Victoria Falls.

And it was here that I decided to be in Philadelphia for a good friend's wedding at the first part of April. Then to Omaha, Nebraska, on April 6th to land back home. This brought me home 23 months after I left, with 23 years worth of experiences. The plans were sketchy after that—but that was to be expected. There were still many more miles to travel, and many more adventures to come.

| *Tanzanian wow* photographs | [121], page 151 | [122], page 152 | [123], page 153 |
| | [124], page 153 | [125], page 153 | |

Entry Forty-eight: Even the angels went, "Ahh!"

I love riding on trains, and listening to the rhythm of the cars rolling along over the rails. It has the power to rock me into a special comfort that puts me at ease.

The train ride down from Tanzania to Zambia lasted two days. Outside our compartment window, the scenes of Africa floated by like a storybook. I gazed upon giraffes, gazelles, and even a lion. One night, from the darkness I heard the trumpet of an elephant signaling our train.

In the daylight, green bush and scrub were occasionally interrupted by small patches of cultivated land where someone was in a battle to eke out a small amount of food for survival. I was content to hang my head out the window, like a dog in a truck, and just watch the places go by.

At the border crossing with Zambia, the conductor advised us to lock our compartment door. I thought, "What am I getting myself into?" As we sat at the border crossing station, we watched people outside running about trying to sell everything imaginable. Their efforts were constantly punctuated by the police chasing them away from the train windows. This minor mayhem was over shortly, but I was glad the conductor advised us to lock our door. It had a crazy feeling to it, and I sensed things could have easily gotten out of control.

Most of my compartment mates had left, opening up the space for myself and a traveler from Korea. He was a funny chap. Most of his backpack was filled with plastic microwavable dishes of rice with some kind of chili paste on top. He was broke, and this was all he had to eat. And he ate it cold. He made a good traveling companion, however. We watched out for each other as we made our way through immigration and boarded a bus.

After a very brief stay in Lusaka, we headed out for Livingstone, which is named after that great explorer from Scotland, who once said, "On sights as beautiful as this, angels in their flight must have gazed." From what I saw, it must be true. When I first saw a photo of Victoria Falls, it was another one of those places where I said to myself, "I must go there to see this with my own eyes and experience what a photo cannot do." Victoria Falls is the mother of all waterfalls; it's 1.7

km wide (that's a mile for us Yanks), and drops between 90 and 107 meters, which is around 300 feet. So much water drops over the edge that it is almost indescribable.

Walking down the path, the roar of the falls gives it away long before the eyes are offered a feast of white mist. Greenery slowly gives way to a vast opening that, in turn, fades away like a foggy London night.

Sitting on the edge of Vic Falls was a humbling experience. The sight that was in front of me suggested that an ocean had come to a great crack on the surface that opened to the center of the earth, causing its water to tumble down into the white mystery of the unseen. The mist rose like white smoke from far below, except this smoke was refreshing. Cool water collected on my skin and droplets formed on the hairs of my arms. Circular rainbows materialized in the spray, providing dazzling colors for the eyes. Around the falls everything was green and plush. It wasn't hard to imagine elves or hobbits scampering about—especially since I was reading *Lord of the Rings* at the time.

The roar of the falling water vibrating through the ground and up my body was magical. I have felt this intensity before in different places and situations; it is always of the same nature. It is a timeless, endless flow of energy that is unstoppable in its quest for its destination. I know it well, and have discovered it within my own heart. When you quiet yourself and remain still for a moment, you can feel the earth shake from the ongoing battle between water and rock. Surely that energy must be magic and touches all living things that fall within its reach.

I decided to explore the falls as much as possible. This included a daylong white water rafting trip down the Zambezi River. This was an unforgettable experience and is claimed by many to be one of the top five rafting trips in the world. As we navigated down the river, we floated over 21 major rapids, in the categories of Class 3 and 4, and one Class 5. I was thrown from the raft two times as we plowed our way down the Zambezi.

At moments it felt like we were in the middle of a raging ocean as the raft would drop in front of a standing wave. Directly in front of us, all you could see was a wall of greenish water heading straight for the raft. Suddenly, the whole raft would go shooting over the top and come crashing down the other side. Instantly the raft would be completely lost from sight in white rushing water before popping back to the surface again like a bobber on a line. It was amazing. The rapids just kept coming, one after another.

The water was warm and the crocodiles were friendly—or at least vegetarians—according to our guide. I wasn't eager to test their dedication to vegetarianism, so I made it a point to get back into the raft as quickly as possible after I tumbled out. At the end of that day my cheeks hurt from smiling. This was my kind of pain!

The other way I explored the falls was from the air by micro flight. One morning I pulled myself out of bed at 6:30 AM and headed out for the small airport. Here I hopped on board a small micro flight, which is just basically a big kite with an engine on the back. Above the falls we flew, with nothing below but open air and eventually the ground. It was a sight that took my breath away. I felt then, and do today, that this view is needed to really gain an appreciation of just how grand this place is.

From above, my eyes captured the entire falls. This allowed me to see things that are normally hidden in the mist when viewing from the ground. As we flew through the air, my pilot asked me if I wanted to go for a ride. I said "Yes" without asking what that meant. The next thing I knew we started diving down, spinning around and around, before climbing back up and almost coming to a stall before diving back down again. "Jeesh," I thought to myself, "next time just say 'no.'"

We flew over an island that had a lone hippo out grazing in the grass. We also spied several swimming in herds close to the banks of the Zambezi. In the river below we could see crocodiles swimming across from one side to the other. It's not the kind of place where we'd want to try an emergency landing. There wouldn't be much of a chance! The flight was short, but oh so good.

While in Livingstone, I visited the falls four times. I befriended the gatekeepers, so they let me in for free after the first visit. This was helpful as $10 a visit would otherwise add up fast. It's truly amazing what a smile and a Coke can do.

After four days, I felt that I had experienced what I came to see and feel at Victoria Falls. I then set my sights on Namibia, a fairly new place to explore in southern Africa, which held the promise of more adventure.

Even the angels went, "Ahh!" photographs   [126], page 154   [127], page 155   [128], page 155

Entry Forty-nine: Namibia

My bus ride to Namibia was like being beamed back into the western world. Although the road was empty for as far as you could see, and the occasional thatched village slipped by, we were heading south and becoming more "westernized" as we traveled. Arriving at 4:30 in the morning, the modern looking city of Windhoek was impressive after miles and months of dusty, dirty towns and villages.

Later that day I suffered a bit of culture shock as I walked through huge grocery stores with endless selections and aisles. It was an indication of just how much I had gone through in the last several weeks—and what lay ahead as the day I return home approached. But it was good to find familiar food again, clean bathrooms, hot showers and even a swimming pool for cooling off.

I took another ten-day safari to explore the highlights of Namibia, a diverse and fascinating country, dry and expansive. The 3,000-kilometer trek gave me an eyeful of amazing sights and unforgettable moments. My seven safari mates were Sian and Alex from England, Will and Wendy from New Zealand, Marc (otherwise known as "The Dutchman") from Holland and Helena from the Czech Republic. We all got on really well. Given we were spending 24 hours a day together, that was a good thing.

I had heard of this ten-day "Highlights of Namibia" backpacker's trip in Zambia. There I met Mike, the owner of the safari company. We hit it off well, so I had a good feeling going into this journey.

A backpacker's trip has certain elements to it that are common through all budget-type journeys. You generally set up and take down your own tent. Cooking is prepared by someone who knows how to cook for groups. The group members alternately share the cleaning chores. And, you generally are crammed into a vehicle with not much room to spare.

It's a system that works, as long as everyone is willing. Our guide told us of past nightmares with groups whose members hated each other. One even went as far as tying a chicken bone to someone else's tent, so in the night the jackals came and pulled the tent to the ground in a attempt to get the bone. "A nice idea," I thought, and filed it away for future reference if needed.

One morning as I was taking down my tent, a red scorpion came crawling out from underneath and charged at me. "Whoa, what's this all about?" I thought. Soon afterwards, a baby scorpion followed its parent's pathway. I gave them room, and off they went. It was a good reminder not to leave your shoes outside at night, for you just might end up with extra passengers.

Namibia is a pretty roomy country, and in some ways reminded me of Australia: miles of scrub and brush. Occasionally roadside I would see a Kudu antelope or warthog, but not often. Some people would have found these long stretches boring, but for me it was relaxing and a chance to read, reflect on my time in Africa, and contemplate future plans.

Will, one of my travel companions from New Zealand, asked the hardest question of the trip: "Dean, what will you do differently when you return home?" That question gave me plenty to chew on for the quiet moments and long drives. The trip was a good break from travel, in that I didn't have to make any decisions—only sit back, enjoy the scenery and take a few photos.

The campsites and national parks we stayed in were quite posh compared to what I had been used to. Swimming pools and good showers had me feeling like I was on vacation again. The game was spread out a bit because of recent rains. The weather allowed them to wander away from water holes, and be less concentrated in their search of food. We still saw plenty of wildlife and had many great chances for photos.

As we drove for the coast, we kicked up dust along a stretch of land that was as empty a place as I've ever seen. Nothing was growing as far as you could see; it was just flat and rocky. And it was that way right up to the very shores of the Atlantic Ocean, where the waves crashed into the sands of Namibia. The ground was mostly salt, and had a whitish color to it that added to the beauty. Things do live there, but they are of the hardiest type, and unique in their ways of life.

The trip highlights included a stop at Cape Cross along the Skeleton Coast. Here we had lunch with 100,000 fur seals and their pups. Stretching down the rocky coast and dotted across the surface of the ocean were seals as far as we could see. Pretty impressive! The view was also punctuated with a very strong smell that reminded me of the hog houses back in Iowa!

While in Swakopmund, we spent part of an afternoon quad biking through the massive sand dunes along the coast. These enormous dunes were like tan waves on the surface of the earth that stretched as far as the eye could see. It turned out to be a very good way to explore the area and a lot of fun.

I generally steer away from these things over concern of what effect it has on the environment, but I suspended my own judgment until later. Once was enough, but I will never forget the sight of "The Dutchman" flying backwards as he tried to climb a dune and lost control. Unhurt, he jumped back on the bike as I roared with laughter at the sight of this huge Dutchman tumbling down the dune.

We ended our trip with a journey into the heart of the red dunes of Sossusvlei. The desert in Namibia, they say, is the oldest desert in the world. It does have an ancient feeling to it, and seems eerie at times as you see trees that have stood dead on the empty pans (dried lake beds) for a millennium.

Early one morning, we rose long before the dawn and filed into our minivan half-asleep. We drove through the darkness until we came to a spot where we could see part of an outline of a large dune that eventually climbed up and disappeared into the darkness. Climbing the dune was a test of determination; for every two steps forward, you slid one step backwards. This went on for about an hour until finally, sucking wind, I reached the top with my companions.

Here we sat and watched the beginning of a new day rise over the red dunes of Namibia. It was magic. After that we headed deeper into the desert to explore more dunes and pans that looked unreal, like a scene from another world, or how you might imagine Mars to appear.

Eventually our time together came to an end, and we rolled back into Windhoek. And once again this nice small community I had lived with all went separate ways, and as usual I was sad to see them go.

I turned my eyes toward Cape Town, and felt the excitement grow at the thought of seeing friends in Europe. Cape Town would mark the end of my Africa exploration, and in many ways the end of this amazing journey.

Namibia photographs   [129], page 156   [130], page 156   [131], page 157   [132], page 158

Entry Fifty: No longer so dark and mysterious

On my overnight bus ride from Windhoek, Namibia, to Cape Town, South Africa, I spent part of the trip riding shotgun (in the passenger seat next the driver). With a dark and empty desert landscape racing by, he told me about South Africa, his family, and about his dream of going to work in Ireland with the hope of making some good money.

The buses of central and north Africa were now long gone. This was a double-decked luxury bus that made me feel more like being in Europe than South Africa. But I soon discovered that South Africa is more like Australia than other parts of "The Dark Continent."

In South Africa I found excellent roads, abundant unhealthy fast food, and shopping malls with parking lots filled with nice cars. Gone were the dirty, dusty roads filled with potholes. Also gone were the buses built for 100 people with 150 people, goats and chickens crammed inside. The roadside shacks serving mysterious foods were also gone.

After hearing that I had never been to South Africa before, the driver gave me a surprised look that could only come from someone who knew a place so well. He could have driven the road in his sleep. He talked about it with a sense of pride and excitement as he listed where he thought I should go and what I should see. Eventually, it came time for the other driver to take over somewhere around 2 AM. We bid each other goodnight. And each took our own bus seat, which served as our bed.

Arriving in Cape Town, you know where you are immediately. Table Mountain serves as an unmistakable beacon informing you, as it has others for hundreds of years, you've arrived at the Cape of Good Hope.

In Cape Town I reunited with some former travel companions that I had met in Namibia. Sian and Alex from England were celebrating their honeymoon. Phil (another Brit) and Helena from the Czech Republic were backpackers like myself. We were a motley crew, good-natured and full of wit. At this point, I transitioned back into being on holiday as we explored the sights and history of Cape Town.

I concluded Cape Town is one of those places where I could live. Here the mountains meet the ocean. Combine this with plenty of sunshine and fine living, and you have a winner. Unfortunately, I ran out of time long before I ran out of things to do or explore.

However, I did squeeze in a great deal, including a World Cup cricket match between Canada and Kenya. At the match, I had a great time cheering on the teams. What I lacked in understanding, I made up for with enthusiasm.

I spent a day exploring Cape Point, the bottom of Africa where the winds never stop. This was the place that was sought out by explorers for years with the idea that India was just around the corner. I swam briefly with the penguins along the beaches, took a tour of the town shops and gained some exposure to the history of apartheid. This included a trip to Robben Island, where Nelson Mandela was "housed."

South Africa is a place rich in history that will take more time than I allotted, thus will need to be revisited.

Unable to slow time down, I soon found myself facing my last night in Africa. I made a decision to climb a small peak called Lions Head and watch the sun go down over the Atlantic Ocean. The view was stunning. On my backside was Table Mountain; below me was Cape Town. In front of me was the coastline with the water-filled horizon of the Atlantic, whose next stop was Antarctica.

It was the perfect last setting for my journey through Africa: rugged, beautiful, expansive, mysterious yet familiar. For a while I sat there on a rock ledge, watching the waves methodically move across the surface far below until they had to submit to the mighty continent of Africa. Where the waves submitted, the wind continued onward and upward, passing by me on its way inland to the heart of Africa.

And with that wind, I sent my prayer of gratitude for all the places and remarkable people I had seen and met. The smiles, the laughter, the sights, the sounds had wrapped themselves around my heart—not to contain it, but to release the African spirit that lives within me.

Africa is no longer a mysterious, distant place but now has a place in my heart. And those places in my heart that held their own secrets of myself are no longer hidden in their mysterious distant places, but are set free to flourish in the warmth of a heart at peace.

For 21 months I had the privilege of exploring a world that was unknown to me. Each day it was my responsibility to search my heart about what to do and where to go next. The next responsibility was to learn and grow with the result of that choice. In this way, the Divine led me on an incredible journey that I am only just beginning to understand.

South Africa marked the end of virgin territory. From there I visited places I had been before, to see people I knew and enjoy foods more familiar. But I went humbled and a little wiser. To this day, I go more quietly but with a deeper joy. I go to familiar places but with new eyes and a new heart. Most importantly, I move forward with a sense of hope in an ever-darker world.

This journey is not yet over, only changing in flavor.

No longer so dark and mysterious photographs   [133], page 159   [134], page 159   [135], page 159

Entry Fifty-one: European whirl

Flying from Cape Town, South Africa, to Copenhagen, Denmark, was like looking at a map and stretching your arms apart as far as possible to have one hand fall on the end of Africa and the other fall on the top of Europe. It was a long ride, physically and emotionally. As the tires lifted off the Cape Town tarmac, I wondered when would the next time be that I would once again set foot on the continent of Africa. I fell in love with Africa, its people, culture and natural beauty.

But it was time to see friends. Waiting for me in Denmark were my Danish family and friends I'd known since 1980, when Peter was an exchange student in Nebraska. As I walked out of the airport into the cool crisp air of Denmark, it was like someone splashing cold water onto my face to wake me up. The shock reminded me that after many months, I was once again back in winter.

I received the warmest of welcomes from Henning as I stepped out of the train station into the clean, orderly and stylish world of Denmark. And soon I was back in my Danish home with Kirsten, Henning and Peter having dinner and drinking the best beer in Europe.

My last visit to Denmark had been in 1987, and although some things had changed since then, one of the things that remained constant was the joy of being with the Madsen family. It was so good to be with them all again. We swapped stories from the past, about what had happened in life and what the future might hold for us. They fed me as if in one week they could put all the weight back on me that I had lost over 23 months!

One sunny afternoon, Peter and his wife Kris had a party for me. I got to see many people that I had met in the past; some were married with children since my last visit, while others sported a little more white hair. It was a great welcome back party, and had a feeling of homecoming for me. We all had changed physically: moustaches were gone, hairlines had receded. Children were tugging at the pant legs of some of us. But the fun and joy of being together picked up right from where we left it years ago.

We ate and drank beer like we were 21 again, except in the wee hours of the night people peeled off with sleepy children and headed for home, leaving Kris and me to close down the fort.

My week zoomed by fast and soon I was boarding a bus once again with a dreary feeling, thinking, "I thought I was finished with night buses, but I was mistaken." Still, compared to the some of the buses I'd been on, this was like going first class.

I left Denmark wishing I didn't live so far from my many friends. They are such good people. I even entertained day-dreams of living in Denmark; I know it would be a good life filled with fun. A beautiful sunset sent me on my way and soon it was dark again against the window of my bus, but ever more light in my heart.

The first time I ever traveled outside the United States, I landed in Amsterdam. That was back in 1985 when I spent a summer bouncing around Europe and collecting stories that would eventually be written up in the college newspaper. That was some time ago, and yet Amsterdam seems to have changed little.

Truthfully, I can't remember much about that first trip to Amsterdam except that there was always someone trying to sell me dope on the streets. Plus, of course, the walk through the red light district was a bit of an eye-opener for this country boy from Nebraska. That aside, the charm and scenery of the city remains; the historic buildings, canals and splendid artwork of the masters can keep you in awe for days.

I came to visit friends in Amsterdam. I got to see Jolanda whom I met in Australia, Rene and Anamiek whom I met in Syria and Jordan, and Marc, otherwise known as "The Dutchman," whom I met in Namibia. One of the gifts of traveling abroad is the chance to make new friends, and I was lucky enough to be able to visit a few before heading back to the States. I spent a great deal of time just walking around the city. Rene took me to a nearby small town from which many voyages of the Dutch exploration of the West Indies were launched.

The Dutchman introduced me to the night life of Holland and I introduced him to the Van Gogh museum—since he had never been there, like the rest of my friends! Then it was time to get back on the bus again, this time for Munchen, Germany, the next city on my whistle stop tour through Europe.

I woke up and found myself in Germany, except this time the bus ride lasted all day long. (You might be wondering why I didn't take a train in Europe. Well, a train ticket costs twice as much as a bus ticket, and I had more time than money at that point in the journey—an additional reason why the trip was coming to an end.)

I had promised a friend that I would come through Germany on this world tour and this was the keeping of that promise. In addition I got to see Sophie, a friend I met in Vietnam, one of my German angels who took care of me when I was really sick there.

Germany gave me the chance to see friends from my trip and from before my trip. Sophie introduced me to carnival, Bavarian style: a mixture of Halloween and All Saints Day from what I could gather, with lots of beer thrown in for flavor. The rest of my time I got to visit with Milena, which was sweet and precious, and the many friends I knew from time spent in San Diego. Spending time with them allowed me to see and experience how much I have changed and the gems that I have discovered along the way. It was a touching and tender time for me.

Then I darted off for Paris, to find myself whirled off to Portugal. On my way from Munchen to Paris, I was struck again by the reality that I was in the west again as I watched a small TV screen perched on top of a urinal.

There is such a vast technological difference in the west compared to most of the places I explored. But it seems the more technical and complicated life becomes, the more separate we are from each other. I found myself missing the casual smiles and exchanges of greetings from strangers. Here it seemed as if many people were afraid, or didn't have the time and energy for a pleasant exchange. Gone were the smiles and giggles of schoolgirls when you said hello. Gone were the curiosities of others, of "Where are you from?", "Why are you here?", "What's life like in your home?" or "Why aren't you married?"

Part of it was the fact that in Europe, I looked pretty much like everyone else. It was easy to blend into the fabric of everyday life. There were countries I'd visited where I was the only white person on the bus or the only person with western clothes that made me look wealthy. In Europe, as I sat on the bus and looked at my clothes, I saw how worn and dirty they had become compared to those who sat around me. No longer did I pull out my photos and have a crowd gather around to hear stories.

My bus took me to beautiful Paris in the springtime. Rose met me at the station. I met Rose in Cairo, Egypt, and she brought me to her charming little apartment so I could rest up from what was, I prayed, my last all-night bus ride. She showed me around Paris and we played photographer. I also got to spend time with Katy and Arno again, fellow travelers in Nepal and Turkey.

I received a warm welcome from the people of France that I encountered, just the opposite of what you read in the news. One evening as we were walking in the heart of Paris, we stopped two older men to ask for directions. They insisted we go with them to their private lawn bowling club to have a glass a wine in the attached bar. We laughed and had fun. The shorter fellow constantly chatted with me in a deep French voice as I laughed and nodded my head, understanding not one word he was saying.

Paris offered a time to reflect, and time to inquire within just how far I had come. These answers were still forming, slowly and softly, into a place of wisdom that could serve as a beacon to light my way. As time goes on, the pathway is illuminated with this wisdom that comes from the accumulation of experiences that are impossible to duplicate, and can only be used to serve mankind from one's heart. Not perfectly, but with purity from a heart refined by the fire of a brief encounter with the world outside one's comfort zone.

Rose invited me to accompany her to Portugal, so away we went to photograph the scenes of Lisbon. It was great fun and a magic time. Portugal has great cheese, great wine and offers endless scenes of life that have changed more slowly than the rest of Europe.

Rose and I walked through Lisbon's streets seeing what surprises might show up along the way. Rose offered one of those surprises, in fact. She got my attention when the waiter attempted to charge us $14 for two glasses of wine and some cheese. They picked the wrong person to cheat. Rose shouted out loud to anyone who would listen that the restaurant was cheating us. Part of it was our mistake in that we didn't ask for a price ahead of time. Still, in the last few days we had already tried this same combination and were paying three to five dollars, so when $14 was requested, we balked. Eventually they dropped the price to $10, a lesson for us and them, I hope. (I was happy Rose was on my side.)

The narrow cobblestone streets of Lisbon were a perfect setting to stroll through as we snapped photos and peeped into the windows and lives of those who live there. The people were generally friendly, and with the exception of the small restaurant incident, very helpful.

Back to Paris we went to develop our shots and see what surprises awaited there. I spent the remainder of my days there with Rose, taking photos, living simply.

My last night we went to a cathedral in Paris—the Sacre Coeur Basilica. I had been there before, and liked it more than the Notre Dame Cathedral. It had for me a Divine presence, a presence of reverence.

Walking up the long set of stairs that lead up the hill to the church, I occasionally stopped and glanced over my shoulder to see the views of Paris slowly unveil themselves. It was like a beautiful woman slowly undressing before my eyes. I allowed the view to sink in and seduce me in the way only Paris can.

Eventually Rose and I came to the church doors, and we slipped in and found a pew to rest our tired bodies. The mosaics, some of the largest in the world, were stunning and powerful. It was evening. The rays of the sun were shining through the stained glass windows on the west wall, allowing a spectrum of light to fill the air.

I sat there quietly, glancing around, and noticed a ray of light landing on a statue of the Mother Mary. What made it even more remarkable was the light was red from the stained glass and landed right on the heart she was holding in her hand. It was an offering brought to light in so many ways, illuminated right before my eyes. A gift of the heart, filled with the light of the Divine, offered unconditionally to me; a reward for trusting where I had been led, what had happened, and what was yet to come.

So many times these messages have come. I gave a prayer, a deep prayer of gratitude, for the love that was watching over me in countless ways, for bringing me to this spot and offering so much. I gently grabbed Rose's hand and gave it a soft squeeze. Then it was time to go.

This part of my journey was over. I left Europe for "the U.S. of A." It was time to see friends and family, to share with them what I had discovered along the way and what adventure does to your heart.

I will spend the rest of my life discovering the magnitude of this journey, but I know this trip will always serve as a benchmark of living in an extraordinary way. I have had the honor of meeting people of all makes and flavors who have added to my own definition of who I am in the world. I move forward with a greater faith in humanity, in myself, and in the Divine and all His endless ways of being expressed.

Eurpoean whirl photographs   [136], page 160   [137], page 160   [138], page 160

Entry Fifty-two: Stateside again

I landed back in the United States on April 1, 2003. Except for embassies, it had been 22 1/2 months since I'd last stepped onto American soil.

My good friend Vic was getting married four days later in Pennsylvania. This allowed me some time to rest, adjust and visit. I sandwiched in a short trip to New York City between my arrival in, and departure from, Philly. I couldn't come to the East Coast and not go to the one place that had affected my trip more then anything else: Ground Zero.

With a little help from my friends, I boarded a train bound for New York City. A roundtrip ticket, which I could buy once on board, cost me $90. This left me wishing I was back in Africa where a two-day train ride was a whopping $18. At one point we switched trains, which allowed me a window of time to head up to the bookstore to get some news and information. While there, I found a *Lonely Planet Travel Guide* for New York City and I spent the rest of my ride buried in that book as I read in great detail what had happened to New York since my last visit.

Walking from the train station down to the Ground Zero site was somewhat revealing. The streets seemed a little less crowded than I remembered them. At one point, I stopped to look at my guidebook when this older fellow approached, asking me if I needed any help. "Yes," I said. "I'm looking for Ground Zero." He smiled and said in the strongest Brooklyn accent imaginable, "You go down this street, sonny. That street runs right into it. Goin' to pray for da boys, are ya? Good for ya." He then smiled and turned away.

Eventually I came to Ground Zero, which at that point was pretty much just a big hole in the ground. I kept looking up into the sky, as I had done some 20 years before. All I could see was blue sky, except for those flashback memories of 9/11 that we all seem to have imprinted in our minds forever. It would make me shudder for a second, then I would shake it off and move on to the next thing.

The entire area was fenced off, guarded by security personnel. The viewing area was filled by people who, like me, came to see the infamous location for themselves. Many left messages, took photos, said prayers and quietly walked along the fence trying to comprehend the magnitude of what happened.

Something good must come of it. Otherwise, those who planned and executed such a horrible act will have won. The greater good doesn't mean revenge or making someone pay, but coming up with real answers to harder questions: How can we all be more accountable for creating a world that can work? How will we live together in some kind of peace, respecting differences and finding common ground?

It takes more energy, more time and more money to pursue this goal, but it will decrease the unnecessary suffering that always seem to accompany what looks like the easy way out.

I knew it would be a transition to move from exploring the world to attending a wedding, but I also knew that the time I'd been gone had done nothing to my true friends and our feelings for one another. Stepping back onto U.S. soil nearly transformed the events of my world journey into a dream state; not bad, not good, just a different moment of life.

Buddha taught us 2,000 years ago that everything is constantly moving and changing. Hanging onto those things from the past only serves to cause suffering, he said. But how, then, do we bring forward the wisdom and jewels of experience without the longing to return to those amazing moments of being so alive, so free? I didn't know. But I did (and still do) trust where the Divine was taking me as the journey moved into new chapters.

I was not alone, not lost, and not afraid. Mostly, I was excited about coming home. I left Ground Zero offering my own prayers and hope, and headed back to a more jubilant setting: Vic and Joy's medieval wedding!

Stateside again photograph   [139], page 161

Entry Fifty-three: Take me home, country roads—an afterword

As the plane's wheels touched down on the Eppley Airfield tarmac in Omaha, Nebraska, I was greeted by Old Man Winter's last hurrah. The late winter snowstorm had turned everything to pure white, signaling a clean sheet for me to return home to. It did spoil the plans of those who had hoped to come greet me, but did not dampen the joy of our reunion.

As I walked down the short tunnel that connected the plane to the building, I felt the sweetness of what it's like to come home after a long journey. Mine was a journey of choice. I chose to be gone and chose to come home. I was not alone in these choices or the implications they had. But I was not sent off by my government, by my company, or anyone else for that matter. I was sent off by my own heart and the greater force that dwells within. The lessons were bigger than me, but designed for me, to learn, grow and expand into God's vision that he has for all of us.

Oh my, have I resisted putting this entry into my trip journal! It has served so well to stay connected with so many, and that part I will miss. On several fronts I feel like the journey continues, that there is no last journal entry until you're six feet under and someone else is creating words about you. To whatever degree this is true, it is still wise to bring each chapter in life to a close, allowing a chance for reflection, and space to honor internally the changes that have occurred. It is in these quiet moments that I have begun to notice the changes within: the expansion of my spirit and the depth of gratitude I carry in my heart.

I received so much from so many over the past couple of years, and beyond. On a recent trip to Seattle, I pulled my car over to rest my eyes and take a power nap. I woke up, and while I was outside stretching a car pulled up next to me, lost. They were from England and their gas gauge read "E." Unsure where the next station was, I promised to follow them until they were safe.

As I was following them, this huge surge of love swelled up inside me. The feeling took me back to all those moments when so many others had taken care of me along my journey. I felt that I would do anything to help them out, just to have a chance to return what I experienced from so many people. It was a short drive to the next exit and a gas station. At the station I hopped out, we chatted a bit, and shook hands. As I departed I said the familiar words so often spoken to me, "Welcome to <u>America</u>." (Insert India, Nepal, Syria, Ethiopia, Indonesia, New Zealand, Turkey, etc.) "You are most welcome here, and have a wonderful trip."

It is the kindness of people we so often remember, but it never makes the news. It is experienced only by those who are willing to risk being vulnerable.

People have asked me what changes have I noticed in myself, or even better, how will I live my life differently than before. On one hand, nothing has changed. I continue on as I have always. On the other hand, a complete shift has happened inside, so deep and profound that each day reveals something new about me to myself. More then ever, I approach life from a foundation of love instead of fear. This foundation is so deep, so strong and pure, that it will withstand any storm, any attack waged upon it. It supports the truest expression of my heart, regardless of how it will be judged or viewed. And it is with this foundation that I will begin the next chapters of my life, with a conviction of passion for life. Not perfect, just true to my heart.

How am I living differently? Well, I don't get so caught up in other people's dramas. I ride my bike more and have started cooking at home. I've also begun taking guitar and swimming lessons. I enjoy sitting on the front porch in the evening and find it comforting instead of boring. I read and watch the news with greater skepticism, no longer willing to believe everything I read or hear. I laugh more at myself, and more easily find a tear in sad moments. I've come to terms with my own limitations, and at the same time continue to explore and expand my possibilities.

In my newfound wisdom, I have discovered a new childlike amazement for life. I refuse to allow fear to dictate my actions in life. I follow and move with love as much as possible, while using common sense to find the purest truth. What does that mean in everyday life? To strive for a simple, giving life; a life that creates more love and peace than needless suffering. I trust more, even when the outcome looks different from what I had in mind. I live more simply with fewer objects around me to distract me from spending time with those I love.

As I moved across the blue dot in space we all share, a habit gradually revealed itself to me. I discovered that I have this habit of looking up into the heavens of the star-filled nighttime sky. It is almost automatic the moment I step outside: my head tilts back and my eyes look upward, searching for familiar formations, discovering new ones, or spying out the moon.

On every continent, in every country, my action was the same. It was my way of documenting internally that we all share this same world. We may speak different languages, eat different foods, celebrate different customs that make us unique as a people. But more importantly we are all one humanity, sharing in the great experiment of what it is to all live together under the heavens.

No matter what so many would like to have me believe about others in this world, I've come to know that we are far more alike than we are different. I've come to understand myself more deeply, and this has allowed me to seek common ground with those I encounter. It has enabled me to find the wisdom to celebrate the differences as opportunities to grow and expand, rather than shrink back in fear or ignorance. These differences allow us a choice to be used either to create more fear or to embrace the opportunity to respond in love. The choice will always be ours to make.

I have said to myself countless times, "You will always find evidence for whatever you are seeking evidence for." I went seeking the goodness of humanity and found it overflowing in every corner of the globe. And thus I was at home in every place I visited. Each time I looked to the stars I felt at home, in the cities, in the desert, in the countryside. But equally, the stars in people's eyes became a symbol of what I have come to understand: This is my temporary home, all of it, every country, every state. Every place I stepped felt like familiar ground, my home under the stars.

People have asked what I missed about home while I was gone, besides the obvious friends and family. Not much, except Red Twizzlers.

I'm learning how to live with the quiet space in the chair that my father once occupied, usually snoring. I believe the Divine had a hand in the timing of my return from the journey. Just a few weeks after I arrived back in Nebraska, my father passed on. None of us expected it. It was another reminder of how precious and fragile life is, and how important those we love should be every day. I believe he took a special joy in the fact that his son grew up to become a world traveler. I miss him.

The future is still unfolding. I'm working on books, photographic exhibitions, and the promise to go explore South America. I am a lucky man to have so many wonderful people in my life—all around this incredibly beautiful planet.

Thank you for coming with me on this wondrous, once-in-a-lifetime journey. I'll sign off just as I did many times on my Web site as I traveled:

May this find you in a place of peace.

Cheers,
Dean

Take me home, country roads photograph   [140], page 162

Production Detail

Editors
> Steve and Annie Wamberg
> The Wamberg Group, Inc.
> www.wamberggroup@adelphia.net
> 719.599.4573

Proofreader and Book Layout
> Marty Shull
> typeshull@alpinecom.net
> 563.382.1737

Cover Concept and Design
> McCarthy Creative
> www.jcm-creative.com

Key Gear

Film: Fujichrome Provia 100F
Lens: Tamron 28-200 F 3.5
Backpack: Arcteryx Bora 80
Boots: Asolo Leather with Gortex lining
Underwear: Patagonia Capilene

Camera: Nikon N80 and disposable cameras
Hat: Tilley
Rainjacket: Arcteryx Gortex
Watch: Casio Protek
Sunglasses: Oakleys, with breakaway sides